Life Moxie!®

AMBITION ON A MISSION®

9 Strategies for Taking Life by the Horns

Ann Tardy Inventor of LifeMoxie

LifeMoxie!®
Ambition On A Mission®: 9 Strategies for Taking Life by the Horns
By Ann Tardy

ISBN: 978-0-9795857-2-2
Cover and Interior design: Toolbox Creative, www.ToolboxCreative.com
Index: Christine Frank, www.ChristineFrank.com

Table of Contents

Acknowledgments

Like my business, this book is my baby. I have many people to thank for helping me bring it to life. If you need more Yaysayers in your life, start a business or write a book. It will force you to create your own team of Yaysayers, champions, and cheerleaders.

My mom. If you are lucky enough to meet her, you will never forget her. As a role model for moxie, she raised me to live this way.

Rob, my best friend and the love of my life. With him the journey is more meaningful. I have learned many life lessons being with Rob, in particular the art of yaysaying. Every morning that we were apart Rob would call me at 5:30 am to cheer me out of bed and towards the computer to write.

My team at LifeMoxie! – past and present. LifeMoxie! always attracts the right people at the right time. I've worked with some fabulous individuals who have made the ride worthwhile, in particular, April Stensgard and Darcy Negro. They exude spirit, smarts, and moxie while keeping the roller coaster rollling. Because of them, LifeMoxie! is a business, a solution, an inspiration, and a true reflection of who we are individually and as a team.

My team at ToolBox Creative. I am a raving fan! From their fresh and original designs (thank you Wendy and team!), to Dawn's leadership to Dan's patience, I swear I am their only client. They are a world-class team.

My team of reviewers. Their honesty, insight, wisdom, personal courage, ideas, and inspiration helped to make this book easier on the eyes and embraceable by the spirit: Robin Smiley, Edward Johnson, Robin Cherry, Emily Burks, April Stensgard, and Sandi Pilon.

Jan King. If you have a book in you, you need to know Jan King, founder and editorial director of eWomen Publishing Network. She read my chapters every week without fail and was the sounding board that no new author knows they need but every successful author has.

Starbucks Coffee. The best advice about writing I ever received was to write in your third place. Live in one place, work in another, and write in your third place. Starbucks is my third place. Every morning I was at Starbucks in Noe Valley, California writing from 6:00-8:00 am, or longer if the words were flowing. I appreciate every grande, soy, no water, no foam, six-pump chai latte the baristas created for me.

Dedication

. . . .

To women and men everywhere hungry
for that life-on-fire feeling!

Introduction

Caterpillars do become butterflies. If you're feeling like a caterpillar in your life, this book is for you because sometimes caterpillars just need a little nudge to get going. Everyone feels stuck at some point in their lives. Whether we created that stuckness or something happened to us that is sucking our energy, there are times when we feel downtrodden, broken, or just fine, but not great. We are so sure there is more to our lives. We just don't know how to get there. We are motivated for more, but we are unsure of the direction or how to even get started. If you're feeling like the caterpillar craving to become a butterfly, this book is for you.

Do you feel like you have a masterpiece inside you just waiting to be painted? Is there a business or a book screaming to come out? Do you feel like you are in the wrong career, the wrong relationship, or even the wrong town? Do you wake up wishing it was the weekend or do you reflect how much you love your life? Do you dream of magnificence but discover you have settled for mediocrity? Are you fighting your job or loving it? Do you feel blah or bam! (like Chef Emeril shouts)? Do you feel frumpy or fabulous? Do you want more — more meaning, more fun, more excitement, more enthusiasm for your life?

During the bubble of the dot.com boom in Silicon Valley, with a wildly successful career in corporate law under my arm,

I couldn't shake this feeling that there was something more for me. I didn't hate practicing law, in fact I enjoyed it for the most part, but I couldn't help but wonder if this was all there was for me. I was the corporate attorney for a start-up-gone-public and as the bubble was bursting I was forced to lay off many employees-turned-friends. On the third round of layoffs, I walked into my boss' office and informed him that I had added my name to the list of people that the company was laying off. I remember a voice in my head screaming to stop the madness and get back to work. I had no idea what I was going to do next – what made me think I could leave a great job with a great salary for the unknown? But my lips kept moving and suddenly I was without a job. In the months that followed, I recall this fabulous feeling of freedom mixed with this scary feeling of the unknown. From this blank slate I created LifeMoxie!

Like you, I am on a journey, and like most journeys, mine does not look anything like I thought it would when I started. In fact, I'm not sure I had any clue what that path even looked like at the beginning. I have redefined LifeMoxie! many times along the way and, as a result, it has redefined me.

In the movie the *Matrix,* Morpheus presents Mr. Anderson (played by Keanu Reeves) with two pills, a red one and a blue one. Morpheus says, "This is your last chance. After this there is no turning back." He instructs Mr. Anderson to take the blue pill to end the story and wake up in his bed to believe whatever he wants, or take the red pill to stay in "Alice's wonderland" and discover how deep the rabbit hole really is. If you are similarly ready for an adventure, consider this book to be the red pill. This is just the start of a new adventure, one that you will define, and one that inevitably will define you.

Welcome to the World of Moxie

Moxie is a way of life. We can create it just like we create any other way of life — good or bad. Everyone experiences fear when they go out on a limb or attempt to step out of their comfort zone, and that fear never goes away, even with moxie. Most people do not step out of their comfort zone ever, paralyzed by this fear. When you start approaching life with this attitude called "moxie," however, you will discover that while the fear may still be there, the moxie is so loud that it becomes hard to hear the fear. Why do some people become rich, famous, and powerful? It's not from hoping, dreaming, wishing, or extra praying. It's not the power of positive thinking. It's not even the power of attraction. It's all about their moxie.

The word moxie has a life of its own. It's slang for strength, energy, courage, and mental sharpness combined. It's synonymous with having guts, spunk, spirit, fortitude, street smarts, and chutzpah! It is the determination and courage to move forward in the face of all that life throws your way. It is operating from a strength of purpose; following your heart and soul, not your circumstances; and facing difficulty with courage and grit.

In Chinese medicine, moxibustion is an ancient form of heat therapy used to treat injuries. The heat is applied directly on the skin to stimulate circulation and induce a smoother flow of blood to treat the pain. The intense heat forces the body to send healing attention to the area, such as anti-inflammatory compounds, white blood cells, and endorphins. The treatment is considered to be especially effective in treating chronic problems and weaknesses, while adding new energy to the body. Moxie works on our lives in a similar way. As soon as intense heat is applied to any area of our lives, that area of chronic pain and weakness is restored, resulting in new healing energy.

Icons like Oprah, Jack Welch, Madonna, Nelson Mandela, Eleanor Roosevelt, Mother Teresa, and Lance Armstrong are role models for moxie. Their lives provide us not only with inspiration but with evidence of moxie in action. Who in your life has moxie? For me, it's my mom. She lives her life with moxie, and a lot of what I know about moxie I learned by watching and listening to her. With no college education, my stay-at-home mom raised three children, managed the family and the family farm while my dad managed his company, and earned a real estate license to generate her own money. She has since served 23 years in the real estate industry, most recently as the vice-president of a real estate firm managing an office of 100 realtors. She lives the moxie strategies, and you will meet her in the pages that follow.

Everyone has had a "moxie moment." Whether we were 5 and exuded this feeling of unstoppability or we did something that took guts that one sunny day. That was moxie. 5-year-olds radiate moxie because they don't have a lot of experience with the word "can't." They don't have a huge laundry list of failures and disappointments they are dragging with them like oversized crates. They only know a world of possibility. The I'm-going-to-be-an-astronaut feeling! That feeling of possibility is what we get when we start creating moxie.

Even after age 5, you probably can think of a moment in your life where you felt this unstoppable feeling and showed some moxie. Maybe it was a time that you asked for the job, made a case for your raise, expressed an opinion in a meeting, stood up for someone else, or took a crazy and brazen adventure. That was a "moxie moment." Remember that time, talk about it, write about it, share it with others. To create more moxie, we need to create more moxie moments.

Moxie is something you will create in a moment. You will begin to crave that unstoppable, magnanimous feeling you got when you created that one moxie moment. You'll look back and think "*who was I?*" and then you'll want another moxie moment. You'll start creating moxie moments more often and before you know it the moxie moments of your life will start blending together. Soon your life will be infused with moxie.

What are you going to do with all that moxie? Maybe you want to start a business, excel at your work, change your career, find a better job, stand out, be more adventurous, be happier, feel freer, emanate confidence, or just fall in love with your life. Whatever your reason, moxie is the answer!

When you are so committed to something you want, it doesn't matter what people think about you. People will always judge you – good or bad. What's more important is how you judge you. Do you feel "on fire!" or do you feel stuck? People with moxie know that the way they live their life – with this attitude of moxie – is the key to their fulfilling life. With moxie, they have created more money, more success, more adventures, more freedom, and a lot more fun.

Moxie gave me one of my most defining life experiences following law school. While I was unaware of its power at the time, I continue to use it as a reminder of my ability to create my own moxie at any moment.

When I was graduating from law school, I was feeling stuck. I had lost my life's direction. Having spent the prior seven years going to school, I was faced with the "now what?" I hadn't planned on anything past the state bar exam. What was going to get me excited about life now? I didn't know where I wanted to work or what I wanted to do with all of my education.

While contemplating my choices and studying for the bar exam during the summer after graduation, I interned for a firm. One of the partners at the firm inquired about my plans following the bar. Noticing my hesitation, he offered his unsolicited advice. He said the best thing he had ever done in his life was move away from home. He moved to Atlanta for two years and eventually moved back, but the experience changed his life forever.

I walked home that day in a daze, stunned by the thought that I had lived my whole life in Illinois. It had never occurred to me that I had the option to move away from home. What was out there that I might be missing? Where would I go? Perhaps California. I still carried with me memories of the wonderful trip to San Francisco my family had taken 10 years prior. When would I leave? Why not right now? And then like the screeching wheels of a car avoiding a crash came the dreaded *how*...How would I pay for it? How would I make friends? How would I find a place to live? How would I find a job?

But suddenly something my mom always said came back to me: What's the worst that could happen? It became louder and louder, and soon I stopped hearing the *how*. In fact, the mantra muted the *how*. I kept asking myself, "What's the worst that could happen?" And I consistently answered, "The worst that could happen is that I hate it and I move back home." All of this in one short walk back to my apartment.

With that I called my mom, and in one of those *moxie moments* I said, "I'm moving to California." Infused with her own moxie, she exclaimed, "Great! I can't wait to visit you!" I hesitated telling my dad until I had more of the *how* figured out because I knew he would ask me all the unanswerable questions. I was afraid that his negativity would give my *how* a megaphone and put a road block in my path. I decided to tell him after I had more clarity on the details, but in order to get that clarity and those details I just needed to keep moving forward.

As soon as I put it out there, the world started opening up in my favor. People connected me to their friends in San Francisco, shared restaurants not to miss, and told stories of adventures to take in the Bay Area. My friends declared their intention to visit. My mom made plans for her first trip. I applied for jobs and received three offers. My dad lent me one of the cars from his business. My cousin spent the weekend driving around the Bay Area with me until I found an apartment to rent. Within one month I had moved to California, knowing that if I hated it, I could always move home. By saying *Yes!* to California without waiting to figure it all out first, I put the wheels in motion. This allowed me to not get stuck in the details of the *how*. In the midst of it all I didn't recognize that it was moxie that allowed me to make one of the biggest moves of my life. But looking back, I see clearly that I had created that moxie, and as a result, a powerful experience.

Moxie is created. It doesn't happen to you. You aren't born with it. You make it, you cultivate it, you cherish it, you create it. There are nine strategies for creating moxie. We'll dive into each one, and you will quickly see how you too can create moxie for your own life. Once you start putting the strategies together and creating your own moxie, you will not want to continue your journey without it. People with moxie actually enjoy their work, their play, their relationships, and their lives. Get ready to learn the nine moxie strategies and get ready to start enjoying the ride!

1

Beat the Alarm Clock

· · · · · · · · · · · · · · · · · ·

Putting Your Ambition on a Mission

When we are excited about life, we get excited about getting
up to take it on. Sometimes we even wake up before the alarm
rings — we beat the alarm clock. When we aren't lit up about our
life, we beat *up* the alarm clock. Do you ever get up early feeling
energized about the day ahead of you, let alone your life? If you
want moxie in your life, you need something to be excited about,
something to work on, something to wake up early for. If you don't
have something you're excited about, make it up! Getting up every
morning to go through another day of work to pay bills, deal with
a commute, manage an irritable boss or a dysfunctional team,
clean the house, run errands, or cook dinner isn't very inspiring.
In fact, it's no wonder we feel like killing the alarm clock every
morning. To get fired up about your life, start setting your own
beat-the-alarm goals.

Most children do not need alarm clocks; in fact, they often
act as *our* alarm clocks. They get excited about activities that we
find mundane and routine. They are thrilled when they have a play
date with a favorite friend, when lunch is at McDonald's, when it's
their birthday, when it's Christmas morning, when they're going
on vacation, or whenever they have a new adventure awaiting
them. They are very in-the-moment creatures that get excited for

the mundane as well as the fresh. This exuberance towards life that we also experienced as children evaporates over the years as less and less feels new.

Beat-the-Alarm Goals.

While children get excited because every day naturally feels like a new adventure, we as adults need to consciously create that every-day-is-a-new-adventure feeling. Beat-the-alarm goals are perfect for doing just that. Beat-the-alarm goals give us new adventures and a reason to get up early. Whether it's a one-day goal or a lifetime mission, we need to find a reason to get up and attack the day with joy and excitement. Only with a reason to get up do we have the foundation from which to create moxie, and only when getting up matters does creating moxie even matter.

Beat-the-alarm goals come in all shapes and sizes depending on where you are in your life. In the summer of 1999, Lance Armstrong's beat-the-alarm goal was to win the Tour de France. Three years earlier, however, his beat-the-alarm goal was to beat the cancer that ravaged his body. One beat-the-alarm goal for teenagers is to pass their driver's test to obtain a driver's license. When they become college graduates, one of their beat-the-alarm goals is to land a great job. For many couples, a beat-the-alarm goal is to start a family. Even companies have beat-the-alarm goals. The founders of Ethos Water have a beat-the-alarm goal of donating $10 million by the end of 2010 to support humanitarian water projects by selling water through Starbucks.

Beat-the-alarm goals are highly interdependent. While it will take a beat-the-alarm goal to put moxie into your life, it will also take moxie for you to pursue that beat-the-alarm goal. Amelia Earhart became interested in aviation while serving as an army nurse during World War I. She was issued her pilot's license in 1923, and in 1932 became the first woman to fly solo on a transatlantic flight. In 1937 she began a round-the-world research flight and disappeared over the central Pacific. In the early 1900s when women were just winning the right to vote, Amelia was breaking her own stereotypes. As evidenced by her adventures and accomplishments, Amelia was already living her life from moxie; and yet it took even more moxie for her to pursue her beat-the-alarm goal – her round-the-world flight.

Create Meaning.

When our life has more meaning, we don't even need the snooze button on the alarm clock or in our life. The problem is that many of us wait in hope that some meaning will suddenly show up. Or alternatively, we spend all of our days in search of that big life meaning as if it's out there and we just haven't found it yet. In the movie *City Slickers,* Billy Crystal's character is unhappy, feeling his journey has flat-lined in spite of an apparently wonderful life with a fabulous marriage, two great kids, and a job that supports him and his family. In search of the meaning he feels his life is missing, he takes a vacation to a cattle ranch in the desert. Through this journey Billy Crystal's character meets a rancher played by Jack Palance who shares with him the secret to life – start creating your own meaning. Billy Crystal's character discovers what we all need to learn – the snooze button excuses will disappear as soon as we create meaning in our life.

There are many brainstorming exercises you can do to start creating that meaning. Look at your passions, your desires, your hopes, and your dreams. What did you dream about when you were 10 years old? How did you answer when someone asked "What do you want to be when you grow up?" When I was young, I wanted to be an actress and a singer. The fact that my voice could crack windows was irrelevant. When I look back upon my childhood, I recognize an insatiable appetite for entertaining audiences – I loved being on stage. That love affair continues today, but now instead of singing and dancing, I speak and motivate audiences from the stage. When my mom was young she loved selling things, from Girl Scout cookies to her homework to her way out of trouble. It is no wonder her career in real estate sales has done so well. Think back to your childhood; what lit you up? What did you dream of doing? What did you want to try in your life? Brainstorm a list of areas that excited you as a kid and another list of areas that excite you today. Can you identify any common themes?

Focusing on your passions is one of the best ways that you can create that meaning. What are you excited about? What obsesses your thoughts? Think about the areas of life that create enthusiasm for you. For example, Samantha has loved writing ever since grade school and remembers how passionate she was about writing for her high school paper. With clarity, she has created meaning by influencing and impacting others with her written words. She is now in the process of setting beat-the-alarm goals that will further that meaning, such as writing a column for a local newspaper and publishing a children's book.

You may be feeling lost or without any clue to finding your passions or dreams anymore, in which case the way to discover (or rediscover) your passions and create that meaning is to experiment. Make your first and foremost beat-the-alarm goal your quest to rediscover what it is you are passionate about. By trying many different experiences, you will identify what fills your soul (and what doesn't) and what causes your heart to sing. You could volunteer at organizations or events, take on part-time jobs, read books, attend workshops or conferences, or conduct informational interviews. For instance, in law school I was questioning the direction I had chosen in spite of my manical focus in that direction. I had carried with me over the years an unexplored desire to learn about the world of advertising, and I felt a need to do something about it instead of continuing to harbor this secret dream. So instead of looking for a part-time job in a law firm as all other law students were doing, I sought a part-time job in an advertising/marketing firm. Through that experiment, I got a taste of the advertising world and discovered an enthusiasm for the creativity it offered. But I soon realized that a career in advertising was not what I wanted. With that appetite satiated, I took my creative bone and continued down my path of becoming a lawyer, this time with more flair.

Years later as I was contemplating a career after law, I again experimented in many forums to discover new passions as well as my next direction. I volunteered at an all-girls middle school in its entrepreneurial program and soon became a co-director of the program; I became a certified indoor cycling instructor and began teaching a class at the YMCA; I joined the board of a local non-profit organization to experience that altruistic world; I took saxophone lessons to quench a thirst I had had to play since I was a kid; and I went on vacations by myself. Each of these experiences satisfied different parts of my soul. Through directing the entrepreneurial program and teaching the indoor cycling class, I rediscovered my passion for being on stage, a passion that has me create beat-the-alarm goals today. In your own quest for meaning, try experimenting.

Rediscovering your passions and creating your own meaning should be your first beat-the-alarm goal. From there you can illuminate new beat-the-alarm goals for your life. When you start creating meaning, it starts creating you.

Your Missions.

Another way to create meaning in your life is to identify your missions. A mission is your purpose for an area in your life – the reason for creating and pursuing goals. For example, your mission in your professional life could be to be the best salesman at the company, the best in your region or the best in the country. Another mission for your professional life could be to be a great leader who creates powerful teams. These two missions give purpose and meaning to your career. One of the missions in your personal life could be to be the best partner to your spouse or the best parent to your children or to raise children who think for themselves and contribute to the world. These missions give purpose and meaning to your roles as a spouse and a parent. One of your missions in your personal development could be to be healthy and to be constantly learning. These missions give purpose and meaning to your personal development.

There are many facets of your lives, and inevitably you will have different missions for participating in each one. When your life shifts, your missions will likely also shift. You may eliminate or alter a mission, or you may take on new missions. For instance, when you get married, you create new missions around your marriage. When you have children, you create new missions around being a family that did not exist when you did not have children.

You can clarify your missions further by asking questions around seven *E*'s the answers to which will stem from the passions you identified earlier. What E*nergizes* you? What E*nrages* you? What do you E*njoy* spending your time doing? How do you E*ducate* yourself – what are you drawn to reading or studying? How have you or do you E*mploy* yourself – what positions are you attracted to? If you seek positions in Human Resources, you are likely passionate about helping people. What E*xperiences* have you had? With what do you E*mpathize* – with what *causes* do you identify? Looking at your answers to any of these questions will help you clarify the underlying passions that drive you. From here we can better identify your missions.

The number of missions you identify is up to you. At a minimum you will have three missions identified at any one time in your life: one for your personal development (this includes your mind, body, spirit), one for your professional development (this includes your career and your job), and one for your relationships (this includes your family, children, significant other, and friends). These are broad areas of your life, and you will likely identify many missions in each of these areas. For instance, in the area of professional development Mary has a mission around being a great boss, a mission around being the best scientist in her field, and a mission around community health with her research. The important part to recognize is that if you don't declare missions that you are working on in each of these areas, then these areas are going to work on you.

Keep in mind, however, that just because you are energized about, enraged by, enjoying, educated in, employed by, or empathizing with something does not mean that you need to be currently acting on that passion for it to be one of your missions. For instance, Molly was hesitant to declare a mission around her passion because she isn't doing anything about it right now. Reluctantly she confessed to a passion for advocating for the elderly but quickly couched the mission in a "someday" conversation. She isn't working in that field right now, so she declared that *someday* it will be her mission. What Molly quickly came to understand is that she is passionate about advocating for the elderly today. Her passion is not something that gets scheduled in her calendar in the future. She is passionate about it right now. It may be that she currently does not have a job in the field or any beat-the-alarm goals that are helping her to further that mission, but that doesn't negate her passion for advocating for the elderly. That passion is one of the purposes for her life — one of her missions. Identifying this as a mission adds meaning to Molly's life. She can now create goals to advance that mission, cultivate that meaning, and get enthused about her life again.

Putting Your Missions to Work.

Once you identify your missions, you can identify beat-the-alarm goals that further those missions. Without a mission, your goals won't feel like beat-the-alarm goals, and while they will certainly drive you to accomplish many things, your accomplishments will rarely move you in any one direction. That scattered energy will leave you with a lot of doing without a lot of going anywhere. Alternatively, without beat-the-alarm goals to drive a mission forward, it won't go anywhere at all. It will remain merely a good idea, a hope, a passion, a wish. When you attach beat-the-alarm goals to your passion, excitement, and energy, you create an intentional and maniacal focus from which you can create anything you want – including an impact on the world. The mission of Ethos Water is to help children around the world get clean water. Their goal of donating $10 million to support humanitarian water projects furthers that mission. Operating with missions and beat-the-alarm goals that further those missions will create the foundation from which moxie can flourish. When your beat-the-alarm goals and missions come together, it is like the right hand coming together with the left hand – you clap. And when you add moxie, the clap is very loud!

Elle was very driven in her life. She defined success by her accomplishments. She got straight As, attended an Ivy League college, and went on to a top business school. The problem was highlighted upon graduation. She accomplished a lot but was not clear as to her *why*. She had a lot of goals but was completely unclear as to the mission of her career. She could easily have accepted a job at an employer of her choice, but the problem was that her choice was driven by looking only for the employer with the most prestige. Her ambition to be successful caused her to live a fast-forward life without any focus. As soon as Elle spent time identifying her passions and clarifying her missions for her life and her career, she became unstoppable and fulfilled – a wonderful combination.

Peter similarly works on a variety of beat-the-alarm goals in his life and in his career as a computer programmer; however, unlike Elle's initial approach to her life, each of his beat-the-alarm goals is driven by a mission that it furthers. For instance, his beat-the-alarm goal of inventing a faster way for a computer to check for viruses and his beat-the-alarm goal of being certified in a new computer language each furthers his mission of being an expert in his field. His beat-the-alarm goal of earning a bonus by completing his project on time and his beat-the-alarm goal of taking his family on vacation each furthers his missions of supporting and educating his children and connecting with his family. And his beat-the-alarm goal of delivering performance reviews personally to each of the members on his team furthers his mission of being a leader by valuing his team members. Peter's life is definitely full. However, because he is working on beat-the-alarm goals that intentionally further his various missions, he prioritizes his time and is constantly moving in directions that he chooses.

MISSION NOT ACCOMPLISHED.

Missions are never accomplished, and they aren't supposed to be something that you get to check off your to-do list. Missions drive us forward in our lives, give purpose to our efforts, help us create goals, and give us meaning; but we are never done working on our missions. We don't say, "Freedom. Got it. Check, check." or "Healthy. Done. Phew!" or "World peace. Mission accomplished. Let's go home." You will never be done being a great parent or being a loving and supportive spouse or providing excellent customer service. You will always be working on your missions. For example, one of Martin Luther King Jr.'s missions in his life was civil rights. He devoted his entire life to that mission. Had he lived to be 102 he never would have been done working on civil rights. In fact, society will never be done working on civil rights. Martin Luther King Jr.'s daily, monthly, and yearly goals continued to further this mission, and he worked on it until the day he died. This mission was one of the purposes for his life; it gave him meaning; it drove him out of bed each morning. And as a result of his tireless efforts, he furthered the country's mission for civil rights and impacted people's lives significantly.

Goal Setting.

My mom always has a ticket in her hand. She believes that when she holds a ticket, she has something to look forward to. The "ticket" can be an airline ticket to go on vacation, a ticket to a play, a date with her friends on the calendar, or an invitation to a party. Every year she plans out her tickets to ensure that she has at least one big ticket a month, without which she fears her days may blend together and turn unrecognizable. My mom's "tickets" are simply beat-the-alarm goals evidenced by reservations or a paper stub.

With our missions identified, we too can now put tickets in our hands by setting beat-the-alarm goals that further those missions. Missions give us meaning while beat-the-alarm goals make that meaning more specific. Motivational legend Zig Ziglar coined the terms "wandering generality" and "meaningful specific." Without beat-the-alarm goals, we are wandering generalities; we drift through our days; we get stuck in routines; we find ourselves fighting fires – usually other people's fires – instead of lighting our own fires. With beat-the-alarm goals, we become a "meaningful specific;" we bring intention to our lives, our days, and our choices. Start revolving your day around your beat-the-alarm goals – daily achievements, big aspirations, small objectives, and lifetime dreams. Carve out time each week to think about your beat-the-alarm goals. What beat-the-alarm goals could you start working on that would put excitement back into your life? And, once identified, review those beat-the-alarm goals every single day, if not every week. Let that excitement fuel you forward and prioritize your days.

Set beat-the-alarm goals by beginning your journey at the end. Where are you going and how are you going to get there? What meaning have you created that needs beat-the-alarm goals to advance? What do you aspire to achieve? What impact do you want to have? What change do you want to make in your life or in the world? What would have you wake up excited about your life or even about your day? You need a plan to get there. Start creating that plan by setting beat-the-alarm goals for your life, your year, your month, your week, your day, your morning meeting, even your holiday vacation. In fact, don't show up to another networking meeting and put that awful sticky nametag on your jacket without having a beat-the-alarm goal clearly articulated. Without beat-the-alarm goals, networking events and meetings are pointless; in fact, most activities are pointless without some beat-the-alarm goal, even if the only beat-the-alarm goal is to merely finish the activity.

A beat-the-alarm goal that gets you up early may not on the surface appear to be life-impacting, but it's likely day-impacting that is life-impacting in the big picture. For instance, your beat-the-alarm goal could be an excitement for your first day of a new workout regimen, the meeting with a potential client, or even a lunch date, each of which are day-impacting with life-impacting tendencies. Set beat-the-alarm goals for your day that, even in small ways, forward your bigger goals and missions. Jane Goodall was driven since childhood by a mission to study animals, but she lacked the funds to accomplish her first big beat-the-alarm goal – to get to Africa. She worked as a waitress in England in order to earn her airfare to Africa. While waitressing to some would never be described as a beat-the-alarm goal, to Jane Goodall it was a beat-the-alarm goal that moved her towards her bigger beat-the-alarm goal of getting to Africa. Both of these goals were driven by her mission for understanding animals, in particular the chimpanzee.

CREATING BITE-SIZED GOALS.

Your success in life is dependent on learning to think in leaps but walk in baby steps. First write down your missions. Pick one mission to work on and brainstorm at least five stretchable beat-the-alarm goals that would advance that mission. Then pick one beat-the-alarm goal from that list to work on and break that one beat-the-alarm goal into five smaller beat-the-alarm goals. Pick one of those smaller beat-the-alarm goals and break that down into five even smaller beat-the-alarm goals until you can open your calendar and start scheduling time in your day for accomplishing one of the smaller beat-the-alarm goals. For example, you wouldn't open your calendar and write, "Wednesday, 2:00 pm – Change career." That big beat-the-alarm goal is a huge leap that requires many baby steps in terms of smaller beat-the-alarm goals to get there. The five smaller beat-the-alarm goals may include:

1. Update resume

2. Hire career coach

3. Conduct informational interviews

4. Research new careers

From that list, choose one, such as "Conduct informational interviews," and then break it down into even smaller beat-the-alarm goals underneath that one, such as:

1. Identify five careers that interest me

2. Ask for recommendations from friends for people to interview

3. E-mail potential interviewees

4. Follow up with phone calls

5. Set appointments

6. Write a list of questions

From here you can open your calendar and schedule an appointment for yourself to accomplish one of the smaller beat-the-alarm goals: "Wednesday, 2:00 pm – Write a list of questions for interviews."

CRAFTING POWERFUL BEAT-THE-ALARM GOALS.

When beat-the-alarm goals exist only in your mind, their existence depends on how long you remember them. When they are written down, you can intentionally work on them and plan for their achievement. Write them in the positive, never in the negative, for we are repelled by the negative and drawn to the positive. Phrase your beat-the-alarm goals as things you want to do or accomplish, not things you want to stop doing. It is far more inspiring to work on "living a healthy life" than it is to "stop smoking." Next craft your beat-the-alarm goals using the S.M.A.R.T.E.R. technique described below. This is a popular and powerful way to ensure that your beat-the-alarm goals and your direction are meaningful and specific.

We want our goals to be S.M.A.R.T.E.R., as created and defined by human potential coaches everywhere. (Check out www.lifemoxie.com to learn more about this methodology). The *S* is for Specific – declare specifically what you want to accomplish. This is the difference between "My beat-the-alarm goal is to have more money" and "My beat-the-alarm goal is to save more money, increase my salary, and reduce my expenses." The latter more specifically defines what you will do.

The *M* is for Measurable – declare your beat-the-alarm goal in a way that we can measure if you've accomplished it. This is the difference between "My beat-the-alarm goal is to save more money" and "My beat-the-alarm goal is to save $100 by putting $25 a week in my savings account for one month." Or "My beat-the-alarm goal is to work out more" and "My beat-the-alarm goal is to decrease my cholesterol by 20 points by going to the gym three times per week for one month." When the month is over we can measure whether you have met your beat-the-alarm goal.

The *A* is for Action-oriented – choose beat-the-alarm goals that cause you to take action. For example, consider the following. "My beat-the-alarm goal is to be happy" or "My beat-the-alarm goal is to be healthy." "Being happy" and "being healthy" are passive, not active. They do not light a fire under you to do anything differently. We can make these action-oriented by determining how you can tell if you're happy or healthy. For example, you may know that you are happy when you laugh. So, determine what makes you laugh and set that as your beat-the-alarm goal. Perhaps sharing jokes with your employees makes you laugh. Then your beat-the-alarm goal could be something like "each day, share one funny joke with three employees that generates belly-rumbling laughter in each of us." Perhaps you know you are healthy when you work out regularly, drink plenty of water, and have healthy eating habits. Then your beat-the-alarm goal could be "to go to the gym three times each week, drink three bottles of water a day, and eat a salad for dinner each night."

The *R* is for Relevant – define your goal as something that is relevant to your mission and the meaning you created for some area of your life. For example, if one of your missions is adult literacy, a beat-the-alarm goal would be to get trained to teach reading to adults. Whereas getting trained to teach ceramics would not be relevant to that particular mission, although it may be relevant to some other mission of yours.

In some teachings, the *A* in S.M.A.R.T.E.R. is for Attainable and the *R* is for Realistic; but the problem with "attainable" and "realistic" is that they force us to filter out beat-the-alarm goals that may not at the outset seem attainable or realistic. The result is that we don't set goals that stretch us; we set goals that we can attain and that are realistic. Let's make a pact to never decide whether something is attainable or realistic until we at least try it first. Rather let's set stretch beat-the-alarm goals and then decide as we go if we need to set other beat-the-alarm goals underneath our stretch beat-the-alarm goal to help us get there.

The *T* is for Time-bound – define your beat-the-alarm goal within a certain period of time so that you are running for the finish line. Whatever your beat-the-alarm goal, the fire to take it on will be ignited by some deadline. Whenever I want to jumpstart my physical fitness, I register for an organized bicycle ride. My cycling partner Steven and I set a beat-the-alarm goal one year to ride the Davis Double, a one-day, 200-mile bicycle ride around Napa Valley, California. With the date lingering in front of us, we consistently met each week to train for the ride in the sun, the rain, the cold, and the heat. We accepted no excuses. Each week we steadily increased our mileage in preparation for the big ride. The training forced us to eat smarter, sleep better, drink more water, and become better cyclists. We were time-bound, and we were on fire! We proudly crossed the finish line after 18 hours of cycling.

The *E* is for Energizing and Exciting – promise to only work on goals that excite and energize you. If you are not inspired by some goal of yours, do us all a favor and cross it off your list immediately. We do not have time to waste on goals that do not excite, energize, and inspire us. Even if your goal is around some project at work and you cannot imagine being excited about it, revisit your missions around the purpose of your work and your career. From there create some new reasons to be excited and energized about that and make it a beat-the-alarm goal.

The *R* is for Review – create beat-the-alarm goals and then review them regularly. Most of us set New Year's resolutions in January by writing them down on some sheet of paper, putting that paper in a drawer, and pulling it out a year later wondering how we did on our "goals." We don't even need to wait a year let alone a month to know how we will do. When we spend zero time reviewing, tracking, or measuring our beat-the-alarm goals on a regular basis, they fall off the radar screen, and our intention dies. Instead, record your beat-the-alarm goals, post them in many places, and review them daily, if not weekly. Get in the habit of scheduling into your calendar each week your beat-the-alarm goals or some smaller bite-sized chunks that forward those bigger beat-the-alarm goals.

To-Do Lists.

Don't confuse to-do lists with beat-the-alarm goals and missions. To-do lists are fabulous tools that make us feel busy and productive, but in the absence of clearly defined missions, that busyness is deceptive. We make lists each day filled with things we must accomplish by the end of the day or week. We then get great pleasure in crossing things off our lists. In one exhausted heap we flop into bed at the end of each day feeling accomplished, when in reality we likely didn't further any of our missions. In fact, we probably spent most of our energy helping others further their missions. Sometimes we fill up our day with so many to-dos that we confuse ourselves into thinking that we have a lot of beat-the-alarm goals. Other times we use the to-do list to procrastinate on our lives. We spend so much time organizing our life around the to-do list that we avoid thinking about the direction we want our lives to head. Suddenly we look up and five years have passed, and we wonder why we haven't gone to school, changed careers, gotten married, raised a family, started a business, or written that book. What do we have to show for the last five years? A lot of checked to-do lists and complete exhaustion.

Achieving Goals.

To achieve your goals, intensify your focus on them. Try this experiment for one day. Before you fall asleep, write down on a 3 x 5 index card your beat-the-alarm goals that you are committed to accomplishing by the end of the next day. As you wake in the morning, before your feet hit the floor, read that index card. Then carry it with you throughout the day, and every hour on the hour, re-read the beat-the-alarm goals you committed to accomplishing that day. With that intense focus on your goals, you will begin prioritizing them over fighting other peoples' fires. You will also notice how easy it is to get pulled off track in just this one day, let alone in your life. Employing this hourly focus, you will likely reach the end of your day having accomplished more. What if you went through your life with this kind of focus and intention?

Another way to keep your beat-the-alarm goals on your radar screen is to share them with others. The greatest ally you can have in accomplishing your goals is another person to hold you accountable and cheer you on. When you express your conviction and passion in the missions and beat-the-alarm goals that you share with others, you will be amazed at how they will work voluntarily to help you accomplish those goals. Once you share your beat-the-alarm goal with someone else (who is of course, a Yaysayer (see LifeMoxie! Strategy #3)), your beat-the-alarm goal suddenly becomes a team goal. They will ask you about your goal, keep you on their radar screen, and support you by sending resources or people your way that could help you accomplish your beat-the-alarm goal.

THE WORD NO.

When working on achieving goals, the most powerful word in your arsenal is *No*. Your beat-the-alarm goals will shift and change as you begin accomplishing them, or as you discover speed bumps along the way. Consciously and unconsciously people will attempt to sidetrack you at every turn with their own goals. Be on guard. With every opportunity that presents itself to you, ask yourself, "Will this take me closer to or further from my goal?" Use this litmus test and you'll find it easier to say "No" without regret, emotion, or fear. You can simply say, "I am committed to completing X by Y date and so while I appreciate the offer, I'm going to pass."

CAN I MAKE A DIFFERENCE?

Be cautious not to get overwhelmed and confronted by the hugeness of your missions or how impossible your beat-the-alarm goals may seem. Maybe you are passionate about ending global warming, overhauling health care, or finding a cure for breast cancer. All of these seem so huge. You my be thinking, "How could I, one person on a planet of three billion, possibly make a difference?" With this it would be near impossible not to feel defeated before you even get started. Consider instead that your lifetime beat-the-alarm goal is so huge that it actually functions like a mission. And like all missions, it is not meant to be accomplished today; rather it is meant to act as an ongoing drive or purpose for you to work towards. What you do each day will further that mission and in the process impact the lives of many. For instance, in your quest to find a cure for breast cancer, you will bring awareness of the disease to a complete stranger. Imagine that as a result of hearing you speak or learning of your work, she visits her doctor and they discover a lump. Because of your mission, she caught the cancer early enough and saved her own life. That you were passionate at all made a difference in her life and in the fight. While you may or may not cure breast cancer single-handedly, without your work the world would not be as close as it is.

Susan B. Anthony devoted her life to women's suffrage; however, she died before women won the right to vote. She spent her life stumping for the cause but never saw it accomplished. Did she make a difference? Definitely. Her work helped the movement grow and continue, it was not lost on a nation that was in the midst of determining women's rights at the turn of the 20th century. Susan B. Anthony contributed her passion to the fight, and as a result, the women's movement moved forward.

People from all over the country flocked to Ground Zero after September 11 because they wanted to make a difference – an immediate one. The tragedy that struck New York City in 2001 gave people, in otherwise meaningless, routine-filled days, an opportunity to contribute and make a difference in others' lives, thereby adding meaning to their own lives. The stories that survived from that horrific period have a similar theme in which individuals helped each other in small ways that made a huge difference. Volunteer rescue workers and firemen from around the country came to Ground Zero to help New York find survivors and recover from the wreckage. Some assisted with their medical skills and some searched for survivors deep into the night, while others served food and took care of the rescuers. If individually they had each felt that they could not make a difference in the situation, they would not have come, and the rescue efforts would have suffered physically and in spirit. The fact that they each showed up made the difference.

A can't-make-a-difference attitude impacted the attendance at a local school board meeting, but the can-make-a-difference attitude of the few that showed saved the night. The board held a meeting to discuss and review the next year's budget with the community and give them an opportunity to offer feedback. Earlier that morning, John had attended a parent-teacher conference and felt the impact of the tight budget on his son's experience in computer class, so he decided to attend the school board meeting to find out more. To his shock he was one among only seven other members of the community who showed up to discuss the budget. Everyone else was either busy, did not care, or, more likely, did not feel that their input would make any difference in the board's operations. John began asking questions and offering alternative solutions, including tapping into local corporate sponsors. His feedback and ideas were refreshing to the board, without which the boards' options would have been limited. That night members of the board took copious notes, engaged in dialogue with John and the other six members of the community, and made plans to follow up on various ideas and questions presented. John's curiosity for the process caused him to show up at the meeting and because he did, he made a difference in the process. Others who felt they could not make a difference stayed home and guaranteed that they did not make one.

SNOOZE BUTTON

Like the snooze button delays our day, excuses delay our life. As you move forward in your journey, be conscious of how many times you hit the snooze button. It is so easy to get riddled with excuses as to why we don't want to get out of bed, why we didn't keep our commitment, or why a dream won't work. Examples of often-pushed snooze buttons include "I'm too tired," "I'm too busy," "I don't have time," "I don't have any money," and "I don't know how." I'm always amazed at how often I complain that "I don't have any time" and then I find myself sucked into an inane television show as if physically stuck to the couch. Without noticing, I've wasted an entire hour of my life. The "I don't have any time" is merely an excuse I use that allows me to avoid, procrastinate, and delay taking action, which therefore delays my goals.

Perhaps what is truly at the core of the snooze button is a lack of excitement we have for our life or our goals, a lack of clarity on our missions, or a lack of beat-the-alarm goals. When we are excited about our lives, we bound (if not physically, then at least emotionally) out of bed each morning thrilled to take on the day. Imagine being excited about Monday morning, a new week granted to us to work on our beat-the-alarm goals and move forward on our journey. When we have no compelling reason to jump, we don't. In the horizontal position we can easily conjure reasons not to move. How often have you set the alarm to get up early and work out, only to hit the snooze button until you have to get up to go to work? Isn't it interesting that we will get out of bed when we have to, usually for our employer or our children, but find it so challenging to get out of bed for ourselves? Our excuse of being "too tired" becomes an acceptable excuse for why we don't get up in pursuit of our own goals, but is never an acceptable excuse as to why we didn't get our children off to school or we didn't get to work on time. When our sole reason to get up early is for other people – our employer or our children – no wonder we approach the day with lackluster indifference. We get up for someone else. We similarly sacrifice our goals for the fires that blaze through our day. We end up prioritizing other people's beat-the-alarm goals to the detriment of our own.

But I'm Not a Morning Person!

It is not a requirement that your beat-the-alarm goal actually wake you before the alarm clock for it to count as a compelling goal, nor does your beat-the-alarm goal have to cause you to physically bound out of bed. You do not have to become a morning person to have moxie. In fact, as thrilled as you may be about bringing your moxie back, you may still find it physically challenging to get up each morning. Perhaps you stayed up late working on your stimulating goal, and you are exhausted in the morning, or you have trained your body to stay up late and get up late the next day. When you do become vertical, however, regardless of what time you get up, the mere fact that you are working on your life will generate more bounce in your step.

Destructive Behavior.

Destructive behavior is often an indication of living without beat-the-alarm goals. We shake our heads in disbelief when we learn that someone rich and famous is struggling with drugs, alcohol, or gambling. Why would they sabotage their success? It doesn't seem possible that Elvis Presley, the King of Rock 'n Roll, would end his seemingly amazing life with a drug overdose. Didn't he love the life that left the rest of us in awe? *People* magazine and the *National Inquirer* fuel our fascination with the destructive behavior of other people. We are puzzled by stars who seem to sabotage their success with never-ending poor choices. They don't seem to understand that they serve as powerful role models to the rest of us. We scratch our heads when the rich and famous engage in destructive behavior in spite of all they have going for them. The scandals may entertain and fascinate us, but the reality is that these are individuals who at one time used moxie to make it, but then let go of their moxie. They lost sight of their missions. They may appear ambitious, but they're operating without any beat-the-alarm goals.

We make choices every day and when we aren't working on beat-the-alarm goals, we too risk making choices that contaminate our present and our future. If we have no vision of our future then what difference does it make if we destroy the present? People who cheat on their spouses engage in this destructive behavior because they are living a meaningless existence in their marriages. They have no vision for the future in their relationship, so they choose to destroy the present through cheating, abuse, or just plain indifference. People who abuse food, alcohol, drugs, cigarettes, sex, money, their bodies, their relationships, and their minds similarly operate without a GPS system. They aren't working on beat-the-alarm goals, and therefore they don't know where they are going. Inevitably they feel like their choices do not matter. Even when we engage in distracting behaviors such as video games, television, and social drinking, we are sidetracked from the present. Instead, start creating meaning in your life by identifying your missions. From there you will begin setting beat-the-alarm goals, adding purpose to your daily existence, and making different choices.

I Achieved It. Now What?

When we are driven to accomplish a beat-the-alarm goal, its accomplishment sometimes leaves us feeling empty, unsure where to head next. Krista felt extremely lost upon returning from her honeymoon. Her wedding had been the biggest party she had ever planned. She had worked for months crafting the day she had wanted her whole life, and she did have the most magical day. When the dust settled and she returned from her two-week trip to Italy, she didn't know what to do next with her time, energy, and focus. This similar numbness often occurs for parents after their 18-year work-in-progress graduates high school and leaves for college. They are left with a feeling of emptiness, the basis for the term "empty-nest." If they have other beat-the-alarm goals that are driving them or even just waiting in the wings, these feelings of loss dissipate quickly. If this beat-the-alarm goal — the wedding or raising children — was their only focus, the feelings of loss will be exaggerated and inevitably last longer. To avoid the *now what?* feeling, constantly create beat-the-alarm goals and have new ones waiting in the horizon.

Michael spent most of his adult life setting money-driven goals. At 20, he declared that he was going to make a million dollars in 10 years. This goal drove him to distraction from anything else. Michael bought and sold real estate, worked insane hours at his corporate job, started businesses on the side selling everything from vitamins to ties to hair products, invested in the stock market, and skimped and saved. By the time he turned 30 he met his goal — he had accumulated a million dollars. He then spent that following year depressed. He may have collected a million dollars, but he didn't know why or what to work on next.

He had accomplished his goal, but he had invested no time in discovering his missions, so he had no idea why he had collected a million dollars, nor had he worked on creating new beat-the-alarm goals. Because he didn't know what to do next with his life, he spent the following few years floundering until he finally spent the time to discover his passions and set beat-the-alarm goals to fulfill those passions.

Harriet Tubman similarly achieved her lifelong beat-the-alarm goal, but unlike Michael, her achievement led her to set new beat-the-alarm goals and not allow her spirits to fall into an abyss. Ms. Tubman rests in history famous for her work in the Underground Railroad, a network of abolitionists working to free blacks from slavery during the 1800s. She served during the Civil War as a nurse, a spy, and a reconnaissance worker, helping to penetrate Confederate lines. When the war was over and President Lincoln emancipated the slaves, Ms. Tubman could have experienced a lost direction, her lifelong beat-the-alarm goal having been accomplished. Instead she discovered a new passion and turned her life's energy to set new beat-the-alarm goals – educating blacks and fighting for women's right to vote.

BE INSPIRED BY YOUR OWN LIFE.

Too often we spend our days putting out fires, not pursuing any passions and not working on beat-the-alarm goals. As a result, we wake up unenthused by our own day-to-day existence. No wonder we drift like sand at the mercy of the wind. What is important and inspiring to you may not be important and inspiring to anyone else. But that it inspires *you* is all that matters, for you are the only one that is guaranteed to see your life from beginning to end. Commit to becoming a fan of your own life. Commit to being inspired by your own life. If you aren't, who will be?

How to Use This Strategy to Create Moxie.

Before you go any further, spend time identifying your missions. Without these your quest to fill your life with moxie will be unfounded. Only with clear missions can we create beat-the-alarm goals about which we actually care. Set beat-the-alarm goals that have you excited to get up and take on your day (regardless of how long it takes you to physically get out of bed). These beat-the-alarm goals will provide you the foundation from which moxie can prosper. You will soon discover that the moxie you create will be that which you need to eventually accomplish your beat-the-alarm goals.

Exercises to Beat the Alarm Clock

- Think about what you wanted to be when you were growing up. How did your passions change over the years? How have your passions changed since then? How would you describe one of your missions back then?

- Describe your passions today. What are three missions that drive you today – pick one for each area of your life: family, personal development, and professional development.

- What beat-the-alarm goals are you working on right now? Which ones further which of your missions?

- Write one new beat-the-alarm goal for each mission you have. Make your goal Specific, Measurable, Action-oriented, Relevant, Time-bound, and Exciting, and then Review it daily.

- Write five smaller beat-the-alarm goals for each big beat-the-alarm goal, again using the S.M.A.R.T.E.R. methodology. Pick one and write five mini-beat-the-alarm goals from there. Get to a point where you can schedule one of the mini-beat-the-alarm goals (or even a mini-mini-beat-the-alarm goal) into your calendar this week to accomplish.

Celebrate Your Wins

* * * * * * * * * * * * * * * * *

Acknowledging Your Successes

As we age, the lists of misfortunes we have survived and accomplishments we have achieved grow longer. But the magnitude of our moxie depends on the list we pay the most attention to. It is proven that when we focus on our adversity and failure, we feel physically and emotionally less competent. Alternatively, when we focus on our accomplishments and successes, we instantly feel capable, skilled, and even proficient to take on the next challenge. Creating moxie requires celebrating all the ways that we have already won in our life, even those areas that may, without some reframing, feel like failure. We need to celebrate our wins and get ready to win again.

It is so easy for us to sit around and complain about or wallow in all the things that have happened to us over our lifetime. In fact, it is the one conversation that consumes most therapy groups, knitting clubs, divorce recovery organizations, and non-fat, no-whip, double-shot lattes at Starbucks. The focus on misfortunes is the entire purpose of the show *Desperate Housewives*, without which the show's ratings would drop significantly. The challenge with engaging in these conversations is that their negative energy multiplies exponentially with just a little fuel. Soon it becomes a game of who has lived the worst life.

With that focus, it's no wonder we become cautious about turning the next corner on our journey. We are guaranteed to meet with misery again regardless of our efforts.

Survival Inventory.

Nietzsche's well-known adage "that which does not kill you makes you stronger" is the foundation for your Survival Inventory. If you sat down and made a list of all the things that have happened to you over your lifetime, you could create an inventory of situations and events that you have survived. As we grow older, the inventory grows larger. We could look at this list and be distressed at our bad luck, which reinforces our hesitation to move in any direction. Or, we could look at this list and be amazed at our own life resilience. We have survived so much. Think back to how it felt to be in the thick of one of these situations. Perhaps you lost your job, you were getting divorced, or a close family member or friend passed away. Remember what it was like in the middle; it feels like this is all there is and all there will ever be. There is no other side to get to, no light at the end of the tunnel. We cannot in those moments imagine a day when the pain, anger, frustration, disappointment, upset, and life ache won't be all-consuming. But the reality is that time does heal, or at least numb, most wounds. You made it to the other side of whatever situation felt like hell. You can add this experience to your Survival Inventory. Looking back we see that in each situation, there is always another side to get to, and always at the end of the tunnel the light is on, if not bright then at least flickering.

The benefit of your Survival Inventory is not to focus on the seemingly short stick you received in life, but to acknowledge how resilient, resourceful, and durable you really are. It is to emphasize that in the face of whatever happened, you survived once, and you will do it again. As you move forward on your beat-the-alarm goals and continue to create moxie in your life, you will need this resilience because the path will not look like what you think it should. Instead of being gun shy or paralyzed with fear that something else will happen to you, move forward cognizant of your ability to survive anything.

Accomplishments Inventory.

As the opposite muscles on your body need equal attention, so do the opposite feats. Giving credence to the Survival Inventory requires that we also create an Accomplishments Inventory. Do you have a written list of all that you have accomplished in your life? Creating an Accomplishments Inventory will allow you to celebrate your own victories, big and small. It is not a list to impress others. It is a list to impress upon yourself how successful you already are in life. The topics for your Accomplishments Inventory should include everything from the educational degrees you've earned to the jobs you've had. Was it not an accomplishment each time a new employer called and offered you a job? They didn't offer just anyone the job. They offered *you* the job. That is an accomplishment. Include on your list awards you've won, skills you've honed, and adventures you've taken. If you are struggling to write this list, start by adding the family you created and other relationships you've cultivated.

Notice that the Accomplishments Inventory is a list of things for which you are responsible, not a list of things that have happened to you. As a result, if you've won the lottery, that does not get added to the list; however, if you did something significant and impactful with the money, that belongs on the list. For example, if you opened a free health clinic with the money, add that accomplishment to your list. You should also add to your list any challenges that you have taken on and seen through, regardless of the outcome. For instance, completing a marathon is an accomplishment even if you came in last place. If you have committed to learning new skills, add those to the list. I learned how to play the saxophone as an adult in spite of an otherwise packed schedule and zero musical talent. For years I just talked about it and finally after making the commitment, I found a teacher, rented the instrument, and began taking weekly lessons. I'm not very talented, but learning to play the saxophone is on my Accomplishments Inventory.

An accomplishments list is not a "gratitude" list. While being grateful is important to your soul and your outlook on life, gratitude alone does not create moxie. We are grateful for things that happen to us or for the life that we were given, and we often attribute these things and this life to a higher power or to the Universe at large. Gratitude assumes that we have no control over what we were given; gratitude tells us to stop feeling sorry for ourselves and start feeling grateful for our lives. This is definitely a place to start, but moxie does not flourish on gratitude alone. You need your list of accomplishments to highlight for you how much success you have actually achieved in your life. We have moxie because we create it; it does not result from a gratitude list or some higher power.

Keeping Secrets.

It often feels like it is more socially tolerated to share disappointments and tragedies than it is to share accomplishments. Do you share with others about all that you have achieved, earned, and accomplished in your life? What about even the small daily wins? This hesitancy to share is prevalent among women. Women's relationships are interdependent. As a result, they often resist sharing their accomplishments with another so as not to upset the balance in that relationship if the other person has not experienced her own accomplishments. And when they do share, they are more inclined to belittle and downplay their accomplishments to ensure they are not bragging. Men, on the other hand, tend to take the opposite approach. They often one-up each other in a bragging, chest-puffing sort of way that inevitably leaves everyone in their wake feeling less than celebratory.

This tentativeness women have about celebrating their wins was exemplified by the college-bound journey of the senior girls on the LifeMoxie!'s teen leadership team. The senior girls spent the fall applying to colleges and discussing openly how stressful it was; however, in the spring discussing their ultimate college plans quickly became a taboo subject. None of the girls shared their college acceptance successes out of concern that it would upset any of the other girls who had not yet heard from a college. We watched as the girls squashed their own success feeling it was impolite and braggadocios to do otherwise. As if privy to a leaked secret, we found out through whispers that two of our girls won full scholarships to top schools, one girl was accepted to an Ivy League school, and all the seniors were accepted to some college. Unfortunately, due to the nature of the taboo spirit, we never had an opportunity to celebrate with them; their news was overshadowed by some embarrassment at their own success.

Sometimes we keep our wins to ourselves for fear of others' judgments. We may be concerned that others will think we are bragging. We may fear that others will think our accomplishment is not all that great after all. We may even be concerned that our audience will not be interested in or supportive of our success. In these situations, it is best to revisit our beat-the-alarm goals and reassess our missions. Mateo successfully left his corporate job to launch his own business selling vitamins, and he was doing well, but he harbored a fear of his friends' opinions about this kind of business. This fear silenced him from sharing about his successful transition. He discovered that once he gained clarity on his mission – to support his children in the best possible way – and his beat-the-alarm goal to earn their college tuition through his business — he pushed aside his initial fears. He proudly shared his success with all of his friends and family, and soon his business doubled in revenue.

REFRAMING YOUR WEAKNESSES.

In a sea of positive comments, scores, results, and accomplishments, we manage to focus on the one negative drifting on a raft out by the horizon. We hear one negative comment, and we let it dominate all other praises that pour in. Regardless of how many people rate my training program as a five out of five on the evaluation, I inevitably focus on the one three that someone gave me, as if that had more weight than all the other scores combined. We approach our weaknesses in a similar fashion — we focus on them in spite of a million other strengths we have. If we lined up our strengths and our weaknesses, the scales would certainly tip in the strengths' favor; however, sometimes we have a hard time identifying which of our traits are assets and which are liabilities. A little reframing often goes a long way.

April was preparing for her own *"LifeMoxie! 30-day Challenge"* (check out www.lifemoxie.com for more details on the Challenge and to read about April's own journey) when she discovered that her greatest weakness was actually her greatest strength. As part of the intake for the Challenge, we began identifying her fears and discovered a fear that her biggest weakness — a failure to follow through — would prevent her success in the Challenge. She has a tendency in her life to get excited easily and jump in quickly, only to find the fire of her excitement die out just as quickly. According to April, she "never stays committed to anything."

While on the surface it seemed that April had commitment issues, we reframed the conversation. Instead of focusing on all the times she has failed to stay committed, we looked at all the times she has succeeded in staying committed. We created a long, juicy list of commitment successes just by focusing on the people, activities, interests, and passions for which she has sustained her commitment, such as her marriage, her kids, her coaching certification, and her church. We then reframed her "biggest weakness." While other people stand on the sidelines talking about life and deciding if they want to even take the first step, April gets excited, jumps in quickly, thoroughly assess the opportunity, and, if it doesn't line up with her missions or her beat-the-alarm goals, she leaves before wasting any more of her time. Suddenly, with a little reframing, her greatest weakness became her greatest strength. Are you busy focusing on your weaknesses instead of your strengths? Perhaps, like April, your weaknesses are just strengths in disguise.

Win File.

As we continue the journey towards creating a life of moxie, it is important to remind ourselves in an ongoing fashion of all the times we've succeeded in the past. By focusing on the accomplishments and not on the disappointments and failures, we become the train from *The Little Engine That Could*, the popular and inspirational children's book from the 1920s. The challenge is, however, that when the path becomes bumpy, and our confidence wavers, it is much easier to focus on the disappointments and failures, as if gearing up for the next disappointment. And then in a downward spiral, we suddenly cannot remember one time that we succeeded at anything. It is in those moments that we need our own cheering crowd – the Win file.

The Win file is your repository of triumphs. It could be a file folder, a shoebox, a banker's box, or any container whose purpose it is to capture your celebrations. Label it "Wins" or something else that inspires you, and keep it easily accessible. Don't search hard for celebration. Keep it at your fingertips. In your Win file, be sure to place awards, letters of completion, your Accomplishments List, and anything else that evidences success and documents a celebration of you. Whenever anyone sends you a thank-you note or a congratulations card for something you did, place it in your Win file. Every time someone sends you an e-mail thanking you or acknowledging you for your accomplishments, your contributions, your hard work, or your success, print it out and place it in your Win file.

You can place your Survival Inventory in your Win file as long as you appreciate the list because it evidences your life resilience. If you relate to this list as proof of the ongoing saga of tragedies that have rained on your life parade, then throw the list away immediately. You need to concentrate on your wins, not on your seemingly bad luck. You don't have time for a focus on any kind of luck, good or bad. There is no luck in moxie.

Your Win file could also take the form of a Win journal or a Win calendar. While a journal usually documents our feelings and experiences throughout our days, a Win journal documents only your daily accomplishments and successes. While a calendar usually documents your schedule for your weeks and months, a Win calendar records only the good things that you made happen that day. Make it a rule not to record anything other than your successes and how you felt having achieved that success. This is a sacred place to celebrate; don't taint it with anything other than your wins.

As your trek continues, make it a ritual to celebrate your wins often. Whenever I wake up not feeling as "on fire" as I did the day before, I stop and ask myself, "What am I excited about right now?" I then force myself to think of one thing that I'm jazzed about working on or some win from the day before that I will carry with me until the next win. Get in the habit of mentally reviewing your wins on a daily basis. And make it a habit to review your Win file, Win journal, or Win calendar at least once a quarter, if not once a month. Consider it emotional vitamins. Refuel your spirit and your determination by honoring and revering all that you already are and all that you have already done. At each ritual refueling, take something out of your Win file, like a printed thank-you e-mail, and put it in a frame or tape it to your computer. Put it somewhere that you will see it every day as a reminder of your track record of success. If you live with others, enroll them in the celebration. Make it a custom to discuss your latest piece of pride, and encourage them to do the same by asking questions about their accomplishments.

THE REFRIGERATOR DOOR.

The refrigerator door is a parent's repository for bragging about their kids. From art projects to good report cards to sports calendars and school activities, it is evidence of how proud a parent is of their children and their accomplishments. It's time to expand the real estate of the refrigerator door and let the bragging of adults begin. Fill your walls and bookshelves with reminders of your own success. Like the shopping list reminds us of things to buy, we need to create reminders of our wins that are easily displayed throughout our world. Surround yourself with memorabilia, pictures, awards, certificates, and educational degrees to remind yourself of your wealth of achievements.

PICTURES.

Displaying pictures around your house and your office is another tool for reminding yourself of your wins and for celebrating. Pictures capture the essence of the relationships, family, adventure, and experiences that you have created in your life – some of your greatest accomplishments. It is the perfect instrument to help you celebrate those accomplishments. Years ago I went skydiving in spite of gut-wrenching fears. It was a huge conquest for me; however, in my day-to-day existence, I tend to forget that experience altogether. As a result I forget the feelings

I had about myself as I bravely soared through the sky like a bird. To keep that achievement on my radar screen, I framed a picture that another skydiver took of me as we descended through the air together. That one picture captures exactly how I felt in that moment and for days following – unstoppable.

THE HOLIDAY LETTER.

The yearly holiday letter that we send to family members and friends is the perfect opportunity to create an annual celebration of all that you accomplished during the year. Unfortunately, holiday letters often read like court reports – dry, unemotional, stilted, guarded, and un-celebratory, or they come off as mere self-indulgent bragging. Worse yet, some people use the holiday letter as an opportunity to drone on about all the drama or medical woes that have tainted their year. And then there are the stale holiday cards with pre-printed signatures and no personal notes. It is difficult to say which is worse, reading a recount of someone's pathetic year or receiving a holiday card without even a note of hello to celebrate our relationship. If you're going to participate in these holiday rituals, why waste this opportunity to rejoice? Fill your yearly letters and your cards with stories of your personal achievements from your year with an acknowledgement of the impact that your relationships have had on you and those achievements. Share with us the things that you made happen this year, the accomplishments from your year. Celebrate our friendship with personal notes. Don't bore us with the laundry list of bad stuff that happened to you. It's not interesting in conversation, let alone on paper. Forget what the Smiths will flaunt; give purpose to your own year by acknowledging the contribution you have made in the prior 365 days to yourself, your family, your work, your life, and us.

MEMORIAL SERVICES AND JOB INTERVIEWS.

To learn how to celebrate your own life, study the situations in life that naturally turn the focus to celebrating wins. At memorial services we celebrate another's life by sharing stories about them. These stories are usually bejeweled with triumphs and successes. In fact, many older individuals reaching the end of their lives have held memorial services before they die just to be a part of their own life celebration. So quickly are the ugly parts forgotten when a life is celebrated at a memorial service.

Job interviews lend themselves to a similar conversation, this time focused on the celebration of professional wins. In fact, if you don't learn to converse about your many work-related achievements, you will be hard pressed to land a good job, let alone a great one. Employers want to know about you, in particular about the things that you *made* happen in your career. Sharing with the interviewer about what happened to you in your career won't strengthen his confidence in you as a future contributor to the company. We can quickly move past the ugly parts when we celebrate our career in a job interview.

Another way to learn how to keep the focus on your wins is to watch successful political candidates. They are constantly focusing the conversation towards their accomplishments and away from their failures. Former-first-lady-turned-New-York-Senator Hillary Clinton was forced to work overtime to divert the conversation away from her controversial past and to her qualifications when she ran for senator. In spite of being the first lady who was an independent, successful law firm partner and businesswoman, the public instinctively focused on her failures – such as her failed attempts to repair the healthcare system while her husband was in office. After her husband's term was over, she moved to New York to establish residency and begin her campaign for the U.S. Senate, decisions that were also riddled with judgment and controversy. In spite of the hullabaloo that follows Ms. Clinton at every turn, she continues to return the conversation to her achievements in business, in office and in her life. Consequently, she has successfully won two elections to Congress, the last with 67 percent of the vote. Like all political candidates, Ms. Clinton understands the importance of constantly celebrating and focusing the conversation on her wins.

Sports heroes and movie producers also focus their attention on their wins, not on their losses. Baseball great Cy Young lost almost as many games as he won. But every time he got up to the pitcher's mound, he had to think about the wins. This constant celebration of his past wins allowed him to win again and again. Tennis champion Martina Navratilova similarly kept her focus on her wins in spite of the many games she lost. Martina won nine Wimbledon games and more titles than any other female tennis player in history. For seven consecutive years, she was ranked the number one female tennis player in the world. However, from 1978 to 1988 there were three years in which she was not ranked number one. Martina did not focus on that; she focused on her wins and that allowed her to win again. Hollywood, in the same way, lends itself to a celebration of wins rather than losses. In promoting a movie and generating hype for its release, producers tout their actors' successes in past movies. They never draw attention to any movies starring their actors that bombed at the box office.

Jail, Ghetto, and School Detention.

Notice how other situations naturally cause a focus on failures. In jail, criminals of all walks of life are housed as punishment for their poor choices. Day after day, individuals are reminded of their situation by the confining jail cells, the bad food, the guards, and the other criminals. Even the conversations within those walls are founded on the assumption that the individuals failed. Not surprisingly, possibility and celebration of anything suffocates in this environment. Individuals living in poverty in ghettos are engulfed in similar despair. All around them people complain, blame, and grumble about their situation. The focus is on their poverty, their failures, and their bleak future. Here too possibility and celebration suffocates.

As principal of a high school, Herman was determined to change the focus of school detention from failure to possibility. On the first day of his new position, he was introduced to his secretary who was busily typing before the students arrived for the new school year. When Herman inquired about the 4-inch stack of papers in front of her, she informed him that many students did not complete their school detentions from last year. The rules of detention required that if a student missed one hour of detention, the detention was doubled. As a result, some students owed the school almost 400 hours of detention, and school hadn't even started. In utter disbelief that the system perpetuated this focus on failure, Herman made his first executive decision as principal. He picked up the stack of detention slips and dumped them in the garbage, declaring amnesty. He decided to stop punishing these students for their failures and start celebrating their greatness instead.

WINNING BEHAVIORS.

People with moxie experience failures, but they are too busy focusing on their wins to waste any time on their losses. Winning and moxie are interdependent. People create moxie when they choose winning behaviors, and they experience wins when they create moxie. And just like we can choose to create moxie, we can choose to create winning behaviors.

Conversely we also have the power to choose losing behaviors, but doing so does not automatically cause us to be a loser. We may have just made a bad choice in our life, maybe even a tragic one. What we do next determines how long the downward spiral will last. We all have experience making bad choices; the measure of our moxie, however, is how fast we shift to making winning choices.

In spite of a lifetime of creating his own moxie, Ray Charles was addicted to drugs which ultimately forced him to choose between winning and losing. In spite of becoming blind by the age of 7, Ray Charles learned to write music and play a variety of musical instruments at a young age. A recording contract with Atlantic Records catapulted his career to mainstream success in the early 1950s. He moved over to ABC Records to maintain more control over his music, and he became a legend in the music industry in spite of his blindness. Ray wrote his own rules, he asked for what he wanted, he didn't let his blindness stop him from doing what he wanted, and his conviction drove him to greatness. He achieved wild success because he constantly approached his life with moxie; however, he was at the same time sabotaging his success with a 17-year addiction to heroin. After three arrests for possession, Ray had to choose – jail or rehab. He entered rehab and conquered his addiction with the same approach he had to his life – with fervor and passion, after which he never touched drugs again.

WINNING ATTITUDE.

A winning attitude is the first place to start creating winning behavior. Notice your everyday mind-set. Is your glass half full or half empty? Do you entertain the word "can't" or do you focus on the "can do"? Do you wonder what will go wrong next or do you get excited about the possibility of each experience? Have you decided that something won't work before even trying? Spencer Silver, a senior chemist at 3M, has said that he would never have done the experiment that eventually created the Post-it note had he read all the literature full of examples that said it would never work.

Take a look at how the word "can't" has become a laughing stock in history. In 1865 an article in the *Boston Post* declared that it was impossible to transmit voice over wires (the telephone) and even if it were possible it would be of no practical value. In 1895 a British physicist declared that "heavier-than-air flying machines" (airplanes) were impossible. In 1899, an expert declared that the ordinary horseless carriage (the car) would never become as common as the bicycle. In the 1920s, the wireless music box (the radio) was rejected by one investor as having no imaginable commercial value. In 1926 an expert declared in the *New York Times* that the television was an impossibility and a waste of time. In 1977, the president of a large equipment corporation rejected the idea that anyone would want a computer in their home. As evidenced, the word "can't" is a barrier for many dreamers, but not those with moxie.

Like any habit, a winning attitude takes practice to develop. It requires a consciousness and an intention to suspend judgment or criticism. Catch your pessimistic thoughts or cynical words. Even if it feels forced, stop yourself and think or say the complete opposite. Over time and with practice, you will start approaching life with instinctive optimism. Without a winning attitude, your winning environments will suffer, and winning behaviors will be short-lived. A winning attitude is a pillar in the moxie foundation.

In the first half of the 1900s, it was a well-known fact that it was physiologically impossible to run a mile in four minutes. No one had ever done it, and according to the "experts," no one ever would. Roger Bannister must not have received that memo, for in 1954 he broke the four-minute mile mark, and 46 days later 16 other runners had broken this physical barrier. The psychological barrier had finally been broken. Roger did not attempt to break the record with the attitude that he couldn't do it; he attempted to break it with the attitude that he could. Had Roger approached the challenge with a losing, this-is-impossible attitude, he never would have beaten the record. Instead he approached it with possibility, and this infectious winning attitude caused others to do the same.

Australian Cliff Young similarly defined a winning attitude. Cliff was a 61-year-old toothless sheep farmer outside of Melbourne whose family owned a 2,000-acre, 2,000-head sheep farm. Because they could not afford horses or tractors, he would run on foot to herd the sheep, sometimes running well into the night when the storms spooked and scattered the sheep across the countryside. Feeling like his work had prepared him for a challenge, Cliff decided to enter the toughest ultra marathon in Australia, a five-day 875-kilometer run from Sydney to Melbourne. He showed up for the race in overalls and galoshes over his work boots. The other 150 world-class athletes, all backed by athletic greats like Nike and Adidas, thought Cliff was merely a spectator. As Cliff approached the start of the race, the other runners were convinced this was a publicity stunt. The ultra marathon takes five days to finish, and runners run for 18 hours and sleep for six. Cliff didn't know that typical ultra marathon runners stopped to sleep. He was a slow runner because he ran with a shuffle, but Cliff never stopped running even to sleep. While everyone else thought that he would quit, Cliff kept going, pretending to be herding sheep during a storm. Cliff didn't know he couldn't possibly win this race, so he just kept trying. With this winning attitude and prolific endurance, he won the race in five days, five hours, and four minutes, a full nine hours before the next runner, and to the utter shock and awe of everyone involved.

But Cliff's winning attitude did not stop at the finish line. As the winner of the race, he received the $10,000 prize but again he didn't know there was a prize. This humble, seemingly average man declined to accept the prize insisting instead that the money be split among the five runners that crossed the finish line after him. He argued that they really worked hard and deserved the prize more than him. The Young Shuffle, as Cliff's running style came to be known, has been adopted as the methodology for the ultra marathon due to its lower energy consumption. In addition, no one sleeps anymore during this race — they keep running like Cliff. Cliff died in 2003 at the age of 81, but only after again running the ultra marathon, and many other races, until the end of his life.

WINNING ENVIRONMENT.

It is hard to stay a loser in a winning environment, regardless of how much you feel like a loser. We need to create winning environments in order to feed winning behaviors, which over time become winning habits. A winning environment begins with our physical space. Consider your desk at work. Is it chaotic, unpredictable, and energy-sucking? Or is it organized, clean, and productive? You want your work space to emit an "anything can be accomplished here!" mood. Clear your desk, file papers, throw out garbage, and introduce stacking shelves to easily organize your action items.

Approach your home environment in a similar way. Is your home set up for success? Does it allow you to accomplish things easily throughout the week or does it bog you down with a laundry list of broken effects? Is it clean? Is it dirty? Is it empowering, exciting, and energizing? Or is it neglected and squalid? Do you walk in the house ready to enjoy and achieve, or does the overloaded list of to-dos weigh on you? Hire a house cleaner, carve out time each week for the whole family to clean and organize, fix the broken things, change the decoration, use plastic tubs to eliminate the rooms of stale objects, throw things away, donate clothes and books, and lighten the load (and the energy) of your home. Then color it with your life accomplishments, and be sure to leave room for more.

Your car is another physical space that could be a winning or losing environment depending on how it is set up and maintained. Clean cars inevitably just make us feel new, fresh, and full of life and vigor. As we allow them to fall in disrepair, so does our spirit. My car has a broken windshield, it's filthy inside and out, it's constantly overdue for an oil change, it's rarely filled with gas, and there is always garbage on the floor and unnecessary cargo in the back. Every time I get in it, my stamina wavers. It is not a winning environment; it's a losing environment. I cannot help but feel less than possible in my car in this rundown state. Conversely, when I clean the car, I experience possibility every time I get behind the steering wheel. When I keep it clean, refueled, maintained, and loved, it's a winning environment for me. I am on top of the world driving my fresh car.

Gold Stars.

When we train our dogs, we reward them for good behavior; when we train children to spell, we reward them with gold stars. Similarly, we must reward ourselves for our successes. We often fail to take the time to reward ourselves, as we run right past the moment and on to the next. If we create a ritual whereby we give ourselves gold stars, we would look forward to creating the next opportunity to earn a gold star. When Rob stopped smoking, he put his daily smoking allowance into a shoebox, and after 41 days he had accumulated $188 from not smoking. As a reward he treated himself to a new golf club and a day on the golf course. You could treat yourself to a massage, a garden tool, a night out, or a spa treatment. Whatever the reward you choose, consider it your own party marking your moment of greatness. Just like dogs and children, we deserve to be rewarded for exceptional behavior.

Relentless Self-Promotion.

Mastering the art of relentless self-promotion will allow you to continue the celebration of your beat-the-alarm goals and accomplishments by giving you a tool to share them with others. You might cringe at the idea of "self-promotion," let alone the thought of doing it relentlessly. But consider that when you are excited about your life, all you want to do is talk about it with everyone; that's self-promotion, and that's being relentless.

Let's distinguish first the art of bragging from the art of relentless self-promotion. Bragging occurs when we spew onto another something about ourselves for the purpose of impressing the other person. It entails a self-serving arrogance in which we boast, show off, talk big, and often even exaggerate the truth in a disingenuous manner. In the process of bragging, we are completely indifferent to another's accomplishments; we are too concerned with impressing the other person. The end result is that the other person cannot help but feel bad about himself, and inevitably he dislikes us for vomiting on him in this way. When we brag, we become so interested in talking about ourselves that inevitably we become disinterested in and disconnected from the other person. We could be talking to a wall and have a similar exchange.

Relentless self-promotion, on the other hand, is merely a vehicle allowing you to share with others for the purpose of forwarding your mission or a beat-the-alarm goal, while adding value to them. There is nothing to be ashamed of about self-promotion. Consider that you are actually doing a disservice when you don't share with the world some beat-the-alarm goal you are working on or something you have accomplished. You have no idea if another person needs to hear what you've done for the benefit of her own missions or beat-the-alarm goals. Your beat-the-alarm goal or accomplishment could add value or even inspiration to their own journey. For example, suppose your beat-the-alarm goal is to become a mortgage broker and while sharing this with your friend Betty, you discover that her beat-the-alarm goal is to buy her first home. Only by relentlessly self-promoting your goals did you open up the opportunity to contribute to Betty's goals. In addition, by sharing, you are now on Betty's radar screen, and she may think of you when she finds resources or opportunities that could benefit you. By relentlessly self-promoting, you give others a chance to support you, celebrate with you, and even play, if possible.

When we relentlessly self-promote, we share with genuine excitement about our life or a project or an experience. For example, "Sally, I am so excited about my job! I just have to share with you. I won an award for my work at the lab." After Sally and you have a conversation celebrating your accomplishment, you ask Sally, "What about you? What have you been working on that excites you and what have you achieved lately?" Relentlessly self-promoting in this way gives others the permission to do the same. The positive energy you exuberate creates positive energy in another that grows exponentially as it bounces off each of you in your conversation. Or you could say, "I'm really excited about my next career move. I've decided to enter an MBA fellowship program. Do you know anyone that has followed a similar path that I could talk to?" Or when talking to an employer be sure to use relentless self-promotion to add value to the company while furthering your own beat-the-alarm goals. For example, "I understand that you're looking for someone to join your team who has this certain experience and that particular expertise. I have just what you're looking for and would like to share these with you. When would you have a few minutes to talk?" When we are so focused on our missions and our beat-the-alarm goals, we find every opportunity to share them with others in the pursuit of those missions and beat-the-alarm goals and with the purpose that they add value to others in the process. That's moxie.

CREATING MOXIE WITH THE WIN FILE.

Creating your Win file, your Win journal, or your Win calendar ensures that your successes stay on your radar screen. Our confidence feeds off of our wins, but when we are busy running through life fighting fires, we risk losing sight of them altogether. As you constantly add achievements and successes to your Win file, it's your failures and losses that soon become victims of out-of-sight-out-of-mind. Celebrating your wins will strengthen your confidence which will result in a winning attitude, winning behaviors, and winning environments, all of which continue to fuel your winning attitude. When all you see is your success, you cannot help but feel unstoppable. Moxie thrives on unstoppable.

HOW TO USE THIS STRATEGY TO CREATE MOXIE.

Change your conversation, launch a celebration, and change your life. Start by creating a Win file, journal, or calendar and begin recording your wins daily – big and small ones. Celebrate your wins by keeping evidence of them around you at all times, including pictures, memorabilia, awards, certificates, and diplomas. Continue the celebration by sharing your wins with others in conversation and invite them to do the same. Then cultivate your winning attitude with winning behaviors and a winning environment. In order to create moxie focus on your wins, not your losses. We need to constantly remind ourselves that we've done it before so we can do it again. When our beat-the-alarm goals are compelling enough for us to move forward, our winning attitude will give us the resolve and the strength to accomplish the impossible, even if the impossible rests only in our minds.

Exercises to Celebrate Your Wins

- Write a list of your lifetime accomplishments.

- Write a list of five things you like about yourself (talents, attributes, strengths, gifts).

- Write a list of times or situations in your life that you have survived.

- Create a Win file and place in it your Accomplishments Inventory, your Survival Inventory, and your Like-About-Yourself Inventory.

- Print out an e-mail from last week or last month in which someone thanked you for your hard work or congratulated you on an accomplishment. Place this in your Win file.

- For one week, respond "Great!" with a huge smile every time someone asks the obligatory "How are you?"

- Create a winning environment out of your car, home, office, desk, or e-mail. Notice how your attitude shifts.

- For one week, start the conversation with your friends by sharing an accomplishment, or a moxie moment you created, and encourage them to do the same.

- Add one new thing a day to your Win file.

- Ask your friends and family for help in creating your Win file.

Choose Your Channel

· · · · · · · · · · · · · · · ·

Muting the Naysayers and
Turning up the Yaysayers

On the journey with our beat-the-alarm goals, we will come face
to face with a variety of Naysayers, including the ones dancing
in our heads. But we have the ability to choose the channel of
our lives and in doing so give ourselves, and our beat-the-alarm
goals, a fighting chance to thrive. Naysayers suck our energy,
while Yaysayers stimulate it. Because Naysayers tend to circle
like wolves, we need to surround ourselves with many Yaysayers
- people who believe in us and support us in our quest for our
beat-the-alarm goals. There is no moxie in naysaying. Therefore,
to keep our energy and fuel our expedition, we must uncover
our Yaysayers and start tuning in to their supportive, positive
messages. We must also identify our Naysayers, learn to respond
accordingly, and prevent them from draining us of our much-
needed oomph.

When we were growing up, our television had a manual dial
that we had to physically turn to change the station. As kids we
would sit around after school and argue about who was going
to get up off the couch to change the channel. No one wanted to
move. We were so busy trying not to get off the couch that we

didn't stop to realize that the person who controls the channels controls everything.

Without the remote control (or without anyone to physically change the station) the television has power over us and our emotions. We watch something exciting, and our hearts race in anticipation. We change the channel to the nightly news, and we start feeling depressed from the constant barrage of negative stories. We change the channel to cartoons or sitcoms, and our laughter heals us of illness and depression. Even if you think you're tuning out the commercials, your subconscious is not. Advertisers count on that. You walk into the kitchen on the commercial break thinking it will shield you from the commercials, and the advertisers force a volume increase so you won't miss a word. And if you have the TV on just for "background noise" and you think it's not impacting your emotions, you're wrong.

The remote control, however, puts the power back in our hands. With the remote control, we can change the channel, increase or decrease the volume, or mute it altogether. We no longer have to listen to whatever is on that channel just because we don't feel like getting off the couch. We can change the channel at our discretion. With a push of a button we can stop the screaming tube.

Imagine if we had a remote control for our lives that offered us a similar power to end the screaming noises we encounter from other people. We could end the influx of negative messages we encounter every day by changing the channel or muting the volume. While we don't have a physical remote control for our lives, we do have the power to shield ourselves from the negative communication we receive from ourselves and others each day.

THE YAYSAYER.

The Yaysayer is the glass-is-half-full person. The person who, no matter what idea you have, responds with "Great! What can

I do to help?" or "I'm so excited for you! Tell me more!" or even, "Interesting. Say more." The Yaysayer takes on each day as if a rainbow is around the corner somewhere, while the Naysayer wakes up each day as if it's just going to rain all day. The Yaysayer seems to operate with short-term memory. They don't pay homage to the laundry list of disappointments and failures that resulted from risks they took in their lives that didn't work. They are focused on the possibilities not on the possibility of failure.

My mom is a Yaysayer. If you ask her how her day is, she will tell you "Great!" She believes that her day is great and that answering "Great!" each time someone asks, even when she has experienced an otherwise challenging day, forces her to emphasize the "great!" and not recount any misery or disappointment from the day.

Herman is also a Yaysayer. Every time I see him, he is a ray of sunshine and possibility. He has spent a lifetime in education. He is a teacher and a principal; he has opened two schools, one just a few years ago; he published a book last year on how the education system harms our children; and this year he is on a crusade to overhaul the system. He took on his health last year and shed 50 pounds because, as he says, he has a lot to do in his life and no time to waste in doctors' offices or hospitals. Herman is 82 years old and each day wakes to take on the world.

Reverend John E. Brooks at the College of the Holy Cross is a Yaysayer. In the racially tense atmosphere of the late 60s, Father Brooks recruited a group of 28 African-American men to join the predominantly white Jesuit school in the predominantly white city of Worcester, Massachusetts. He felt opening the doors to them was not enough; he knew he had to provide them with ongoing emotional support and mentoring. When racial tensions came to head in the fall of 1969 and his students were unjustly expelled, it was Father Brooks who brokered an amnesty for the students. Impacting these young men with his yaysaying, Father Brooks graduated from this group U.S. Supreme Court Justice Clarence Thomas; Theodore V. Wells Jr., a star litigator and 2006 *National Law Journal* Lawyer of the Year; Edward P. Jones, Pulitzer-Prize winning author; Stanley E. Grayson, a New York City deputy mayor turned investment banker; and Eddie J. Jenkins, a former Miami Dolphins running back. Each of the men remembers Father Brooks as their mentor, recalling how he gave them time, respect, and the freedom to be themselves. He pushed them to exceed the already high academic standards at Holy Cross, and in so doing, this Yaysayer transformed these men into confident leaders.

5-year-olds with their very short lifetime of experiences are also Yaysayers. To them the world is one big possibility. While they have received naysaying messages from their parents, for most of those five years they don't fully comprehend them. As they get older, they begin internalizing those naysaying messages ("Get down. You're going to get hurt." "Don't touch that." "Stop running." "Don't do that." "Let me do that for you, it's too hard."), so they become more cautious and begin hesitating before taking risks. Also, as they grow, they come to experience their own failures and mistakes when they try new things. Their parents' response to their failures will determine how soon and how confidently they will try again.

Observe 5-year-olds when you can. Watch their unabashed, yaysaying approach to the world. They'll dance in line at the grocery store, while the rest of us slump to the counter; they'll bolt from one location to another, while the rest of us lumber behind; and they'll sing loudly indoors, while the rest of us look around apologetically for the noise. They say what they want, when they want it and to whomever they want.

Henny, the 5-year-old daughter of my friend, is full of life and yaysaying. She will try anything, propel herself off anything, and talk to anyone. She does not care what others think of her. After spending an enjoyable evening with Henny playing games and laughing together, I headed to the door to leave. Henny ran up and gave me a hug and a kiss on the cheek and announced at the top of her lungs, "I love you! I'm going to marry you!" This was her expression of joy and appreciation for our time together. She didn't know that anything was funny about her statement. Sadly, over the next 10 years, she will hear messages about how she should not act this way, should not be so loud, should calm down, and how people just don't express joy and appreciation in this way. Naysayers in the world will chip away at her beautiful spirit. For now, all I can do is adore and cheer her on, and encourage her mom to do the same.

Sometimes yaysaying shows up in fleeting moments instead of resting in the fiber of our bones. These are fair weather Yaysayers – they'll be positive and supportive about you and your idea one day and completely unsupportive the next. Usually fair weather Yaysayers are dictated by their own emotions. When they feel good about themselves, they'll feel good about you. When they feel crappy about themselves, you'll know it. Be cautious of these Yaysayers. Without knowing their emotional state that day, you could walk into a conversation ripe with landmines.

The power of the Yaysayer to impact individuals and change the course of history is remarkable, as demonstrated by the lives of Eleanor Roosevelt and Helen Keller. One of Eleanor Roosevelt's most significant Yaysayers was Mademoiselle Marie Souvestre, headmistress of Allenswood, an all-girls boarding school outside of London where Eleanor was sent to study. Eleanor came to school a shy, lonely, isolated young woman clearly impacted by her disapproving grandmother who dismissed Eleanor as not classy enough to be a Roosevelt. Mlle Souvestre opened up the world to Eleanor, introducing her to social justice, history, and literature. Through her yaysaying, she helped Eleanor gain the confidence and the skills she needed to express her opinions clearly and eloquently to her family back in the States.

As a blind and deaf child, Helen Keller similarly began her life in isolation and loneliness. By the time Helen was 7, her family had fumbled as much as they could on their own, but she had become a spoiled girl and too much for them to handle. After seeking out specialists, they were introduced to Anne Sullivan, who became Helen's teacher for 49 years. She immediately instilled discipline in Helen and then gave her the power to read, listen, and speak through her hands. As a result of Anne's influence and yaysaying, Helen became, at the age of 24, the first deaf and blind college graduate when she graduated *magna cum laude* from Radcliffe College (the women's Harvard).

The Naysayer.

If I asked you to name someone in your life who, no matter what idea you present, has a reason that it won't work, you could probably identify a person instantly. This is the Naysayer. The glass-is-half-empty person. The person who rains on your parade one time or rains on it constantly. Sometimes we cross paths with these people once, and that's enough. Sometimes people in our lives become Naysayers, as if plucked from the movie *Invasion of the Body Snatchers.* Sometimes we are related to these people. Sometimes we are married to them. Whatever the situation, we need to find a way to change the channel that receives their reception or use the mute button to stop the negative impact these people have on us. Their negativity is like the kryptonite Superman spent his cartoon life dodging. We must do the same. We waste our energy when we set out to stop their naysaying or change their minds or their outlook on life. We need to preserve that energy to accomplish our beat-the-alarm goals.

Even famously successful people have endured their share of Naysayers. The childhood music teacher of master composer Beethoven once told him that as a composer, Beethoven was hopeless. The father of Charles Darwin, the originator of evolution theory, told Darwin that he would amount to nothing and eventually would disgrace himself and the entire family. Even Albert Einstein, arguably one of the greatest physicists of all time, was forced to combat naysaying to allow his gifts to shine. He did not speak until he was four years old and even then it was with a stammer until he was nine. Labeling him retarded, his parents and teachers asked Einstein to quit high school. Each of these individuals had to find ways to stop the impact of these negative messages in order to create their greatness.

THE ART OF NAYSAYING.

Naysaying can take many forms. It could be words that the Naysayer uses, such as "That's never going to work" or "Have you thought through all of this?" or "What are you going to do when that idea fails?" Naysaying could be in the tone of their voice – harsh, loud, growling or even the questioning fluctuation in pitch as if they were the parent and we the child. Naysaying can even be more subtle, such as the roll of the eyes, a furrow or raise of the eyebrows, a narrowing of the eyes, or a pucker of the lips. Naysaying could even show up in the form of the silent treatment, a cold shoulder, or complete disregard for you.

Sometimes naysaying is evidenced by joking or making fun of you or your ideas. This often happens in close relationships like with a family member or a spouse because the person feels they know you well enough to poke fun at you. To attempt to repair any hurt feelings, the comedian tacks on the words "I'm just kidding" to the end of the ribbing, as if that makes it okay. Remember, though, that many serious words are said in jest. So, while they try to smooth their delivery, they are conveying their opinion. And even if you both laugh at whatever trait you have that is the subject of ridicule, the inevitable impact will be felt by your self-esteem.

Allison has a tendency to overcommit but never reach the finish line. Her husband is unconditionally supportive of her and her exploration of various passions, and yet, every time she brings a new idea to him, he pokes fun at how he's heard this tune before. Jokingly he says, "Let's place bets on how long this one will last." She laughs as well because she knows her track record has proven him correct; however, inevitably his comments chip away at her self-respect before she even starts down a path. Her husband is a Yaysayer with Naysayer tendencies. Once she pointed this out to him and requested his support in spite of her history, he was able to be a 100 percent Yaysayer to her.

Naysaying even occurs when we witness the negative approach that other people have towards their own lives. My mom calls these people in her office the doom-and-gloomers. They walk around the office telling anyone who will listen what happened to them. Each time they recount the story, it's as if they make the incident happen all over again. Inevitably, this practice depresses the storyteller as well as their audience.

Another example of living a naysaying life can be found in Albert's parents. They live each day naysaying. They live as if they are sick and dying; they've lived with this mentality for 20 years. Life for them revolves around doctor visits, illnesses, and funerals. They begin most conversations by relating some tragic story that happened to them or someone they know. Without fail, whenever Albert presents an idea to them for a fun day, their response is, "I don't think so. We're so tired." They have an especial dislike for experiencing new things. As a result of their negative approach, Albert struggles not to lose his own energy and excitement around them. He hesitates sharing ideas with them because he knows they will have a reason not to participate. They operate from a lifetime of disappointment, regret, and disenchantment that proves beyond a reasonable doubt in their minds that something new will always result in more of the same.

Naysaying also shows up when it feels like the whole world is saying "No." Sandra Day O'Connor must have felt the world saying "No" after graduating at the top of her law school class at Stanford University. Because she was a woman in the legal profession in the early 1950s, no firm would hire her in spite of her seven years of higher education and amazing academic performance. One firm did offer her a legal secretary position. She responded to this mass naysaying by entering public service as a deputy county attorney, thus beginning her legal career in the government. In late 1960s Ms. O'Connor was appointed to the Arizona State Senate, went on to become the first woman to serve as a state senate majority leader in any state, and then served as a judge in the Superior Court and the Appeals Court in Arizona. In 1981 she became the first woman to serve on the Supreme Court of the United States, a position she held for 20 years. In the face of a lot of naysaying, Sandra Day O'Connor changed the channel and ultimately changed history.

Naysaying does not have to come from a person. Content in the magazines we read, the movies we watch, and the music we listen to has the ability to negatively impact our outlook. For instance, years ago I found myself constantly feeling disheartened after reading certain magazines. I discovered that I was engrossed in the pages of other people's lives wishing my hair was so straight, my thighs so slim, my make-up so perfect, my outfits so trendy, and my life so glamorous. These messages fueled my own naysaying. I wasn't inspired to become one of them; instead the publication left me with the feeling that my life was inadequate because it wasn't on the pages of these magazines. Not all magazines have this impact, but consider eliminating from your literary diet the ones that do, and watch your spirits soar.

Similarly, television shows, music, and movies that do not inspire you to greatness should be struck from your schedule. For example, I stopped watching the television show *Married with Children* because it began to depress me. The ongoing verbal battles among each of the show's family members caused me to fear creating a family of my own. We do not have time to soak up naysaying messages, regardless of their form or their origin; combating them sucks our energy that is needed elsewhere. Meg Ryan once shared with Oprah in an interview that she never reads her critics' reviews. She doesn't want to waste time repairing the damage that negative comments will inevitably have on her confidence and her spirit. Likewise, consider any source carrying negative comments to be a Naysayer and treat it accordingly. Change the channel on these forms of entertainment and you will rescue your moxie once again from social sabotage.

Taking Stock of Your Naysayers.

Make a list. Who in your life is a Naysayer to you? Maybe not a Naysayer in general or to other people, but they are a Naysayer to you — that's all that matters. All too often our conversations with some people become engrained with intoxicating patterns. These everyday conversations are so close to us that we can't even see the damage they cause. With whom in your life do you hesitate sharing things? Who in your life is the first to present you with all the reasons that your idea will not work? Take stock of these Naysayers. You don't need to eliminate these people from your life; you need to eliminate the impact their naysaying has on you. The best way to do this is to learn to listen to them without soaking in their negativity and to prepare responses to their concerns. But first spend time identifying the culprits.

Deflecting Bullets.

People with moxie have indestructible bracelets like Wonder Woman, and when the naysaying is thrust at them like speeding bullets, their arms go up to deflect the bullets. As you begin creating your moxie, envision your own Wonder Woman bracelets from which all negativity will be deflected.

John Grisham, Walt Disney, and F.W. Woolworth knew how to deflect bullets. John Grisham, best-selling author of legal thrillers, including *A Time to Kill,* endured 16 rejections of his first novel by literary agents and 12 rejections from publishing houses. He didn't have poor writing abilities; he had put his manuscript in front of people with small visions. Walt Disney was fired by a newspaper editor who claimed that Walt lacked good ideas. He didn't lack good ideas; he lacked the right audience. F.W. Woolworth, founder of the famous five-and-dime store Woolworth's, worked in a dry goods store when he was 21. However, his employer would not allow him to wait on customers because he felt F.W. did not have enough customer sense. Again, he didn't lack good sense; he was in the wrong store! All three of these men emanated moxie. They believed in themselves and their work, they focused on their beat-the-alarm goals, they deflected the bullets of these Naysayers, and they went on to greatness.

It is always amazing that we can spend our whole life working to like ourselves and then one date with a guy who doesn't ask us out for date number two suddenly puts into question all of our hard work. Or we allow one negative comment or opinion from a boss or a complete stranger to mean more than our own opinion of ourselves. It's as if we hand over to these people the right to tell us how we should feel about ourselves, and then we listen to them.

Luckily Fred Astaire and Marilyn Monroe refused to hand over the right to impact their self-esteem to the Naysayers they encountered in Hollywood. In 1928 a producer viewed Fred Astaire's screen test and noted that Fred cannot act, he cannot sing, he's balding, and he can barely dance. And in 1947, Marilyn Monroe was dropped by 20th Century Fox one year into her contract because they thought she was unattractive. With moxie in tow they deflected the bullets from these Naysayers and moved forward with their beat-the-alarm goals.

Stop Convincing the Naysayer.

Here's the trick when it comes to Naysayers — stop trying to convince them. We exert way too much energy trying to defend our choices or convince the Naysayers that something we want to try is a good idea. But there is no convincing Naysayers, so stop wasting your energy. Instead, have a response ready for when their naysaying hits. You simply could say "Thanks for sharing" and leave it at that. Know that they love you and don't want to see you get hurt, in which case a "Thanks for your concern" is appropriate. Or, they're jealous and don't understand why you are moving forward in your life when they aren't moving forward in theirs, in which case a "Thanks for letting me know" works just as well. Just because they are a wandering generality doesn't mean that you need to be one. Walk away and let the Naysayer sort out their own emotions or justify their small-minded view of the world.

Sometimes we can anticipate a Naysayer's naysaying, in which case, we should address it head on before they even have the opportunity to naysay. For instance, you could say, "I know that you are concerned about my safety because you love me so much. I have decided to move to New York to pursue a career in theater. I know it's a long shot, but I need to give it a try. I promise to be careful. I could really use your support." Or in the case of Allison and her Yaysayer-with-Naysayer-tendencies husband, "I know I don't often follow through on my ideas. I'm committed to making this one successful, and I could really use your support." Know their concerns and put them on the table with a response before they even have time to impart their negativity cloaked in wisdom or concern.

Behind the Curtain.

People aren't by nature mean-spirited, so there must be some other reason for their naysaying. The secret to changing our relationship to Naysayers is to understand that their naysaying results from a variety of their own emotions that they're imposing on us: their love, their fears, or their own feelings of obligation. Parents are often guilty of the first one. They love us so much that they don't want us to get hurt. So they use their naysaying to warn us of what could go wrong. They don't see it as squelching our spirit or our dreams; they see it as protecting us. For example, "It's so dangerous in that part of town. I don't think it's a good idea for you to volunteer for that shelter. Don't they have other people who can volunteer?" or "Are you sure that's a good idea? There is a lot of competition out there." Or "But you have such a great job right now. Why would you want to give that up?"

The other emotion, fear, rears its ugly head whenever someone is confronted by our own progress. Our excitement about our life causes them to look at their life. Our forward motion compared to their stagnation puts into question their own approach to life. If you are making changes but they are not, they question whether they are doing life incorrectly. Perhaps they don't want to be left behind, but they also aren't ready to change. Or they could never imagine taking the kinds of risks that you are taking. Could they be doing life wrong? Should they be making changes and taking risks? But if they don't want to or are afraid of doing so, then they need to justify their path by tainting yours.

No one likes to feel wrong about how they live their life, so instead they will make you wrong about your choices. Their naysaying comments are actually concealing their deep-seeded fear of, or plain unwillingness to, move forward or make changes. They may be unhappy with their lives, but they are not willing to do anything about it. Obviously, they are not in the same place on the journey that you are. Instead of facing their fear or taking action, they'll go to great lengths to make you wrong. This abdicates their need to do any work on themselves, their lives, or their dreams. Naysaying results when others have not dealt with their own lives. While you may bear the brunt of their reaction, remember that it actually has nothing to do with you. For example, an editor once told Louisa May Alcott, author of *Little Women* and numerous other novels, that she would never write anything that people would like. How did the editor know that Ms. Alcott would never write anything that people would like, even if he disliked her current work? Why would he strive to destroy her spirit in that way? Perhaps it was easier for him to bring down her hopes than face the fact that he had not completed his own novel.

Tom was married to a woman who was not happy with her life. He was filled with possibility and excitement about his life, but he allowed her to choke it with her own fear masqueraded in naysaying. He wanted to go back to school to become a teacher but she said "Grow up. You are an adult now, and you have responsibilities. You're not going back to school. You need to continue to support me and the kids." Her fear of his spreading his wings when she wasn't brave enough to do the same was too much for her. If she was a Yaysayer, as spouses should be for each other, she could have said, "I'm so thrilled that you are finally ready to follow your lifelong dream. I'm so proud of you! Let's sit down and see what changes we would need to make financially and as a family to make it work." However, she could only have been this for him if she was this for herself, and that would have required her to figure out her own missions and set her own beat-the-alarm goals. She wasn't ready to do that, but she also didn't want to get left behind.

Feelings of guilt and obligation similarly cause naysaying, especially in ourselves. We want to do one thing, but we are torn by the something else that feels like the "right thing to do" for someone else. We work so hard to make everyone else happy that our inner spirit becomes confined in a straight jacket of "should haves." For example, Maggie really wants to quit her job at the family business and travel the world, but the obligation she feels towards her family stops her from even considering the possibility. She squelches this dream of hers out of an obligation to keep her family happy, even though she feels anything but.

You the Naysayer.

Sometimes *we* are the Naysayer. We emotionally and verbally beat up ourselves and others. We yell at ourselves for screwing up and then recall the litany of screw-ups that we have caused over our lifetime. We berate ourselves using language we would only use on our worst enemy. Similarly, when we yell at other people for mistakes they've made, we recount all the mistakes they've made in the past. We are even Naysayers when we innocently gossip or gripe with others about all the dreadful things that have happened to us or people we know. This naysaying about life inevitably brings down our spirits. When talking to ourselves or others, remember that every conversation either contributes to or contaminates that relationship and our spirits. People with moxie use conversations to contribute to relationships with themselves and with others.

When you are in a situation where you are the Naysayer, there are a few things you can do to snap out of it and turn yourself into your biggest fan. First, walk away and distract yourself from the internal naysaying. Go to the store and run errands, go to the gym and exhaust yourself on the treadmill, go to the movies and engross yourself in a fictional world. Whatever you do, just walk away from the victim of your beatings, whether it's you or someone else.

Next, write down all the things that you've done in the past week or month that are worth celebrating. If you struggle with this, call a Yaysayer on your list and ask for their help in making your list. You could also open your Win file and listen to the cheering that erupts from the pages.

Now, force yourself to make only glass-is-half-full comments even when you don't feel like it. Your response to every "How are you?" should be "Wonderful!" Soon with enough "Wonderfuls!" you will start to feel like your response. If you continue to answer the question with "Horrible and let me tell you why," you will continue to feel horrible.

Finally, have a response ready for yourself as you do with other Naysayers. This may sound like "I know this sucks, but let's remember our goals." or "I know it's going to be challenging, but you've done wonders in the past. You can do it again." This may sound cheesy or hokey, but it's better than the alternative conversations we usually have with ourselves in these situations.

Be prepared for your own naysaying, as it's inevitable that you will falter into this territory at various points on your journey, sometimes daily. Everyone falters; people with moxie have just learned how to move through it faster. The objective is to snap out of naysaying moments quickly and to make the visits to this mindset few and far between.

Changing the Channel.

My sister was forced to change the channel after my dad's naysaying continued impacting her even after his death. When my sister was looking for a job after college, she approached my dad about working at his industrial roofing company. She wanted to learn the business, an all-male, tar-laden, filthy, old-boys-club business. My dad, always the Naysayer, was hesitant to give her anything more than the office manager position. In addition, he was a yeller. With every mistake she made, she would cringe because she knew his war path well. My sister not only tuned in to a very toxic channel, she forgot where she put the remote control!

A few years after she started working for him, my dad fought stage 4 cancer but lost. He had not put a succession plan in place at the business; and my sister, the office manager, was the only one in the family who knew anything about his company. The rest of us sat her down after the funeral and handed over the company reigns to her; we declared that she was now in charge of the family business. We forced her to change the channel. She was no longer allowed to listen to the messages that the biggest Naysayer in her life had left in her head; instead she was going to listen to her Yaysayers. We all worked together to prepare and train her to take on this new role confidently. We talked with her for hours on end about how to run a business, hold business meetings, command respect, read financial statements, and lead a company. She stepped into that role, embraced it with everything she had, and successfully ran the business for almost two years before we all decided it was time to sell it. We forced my sister to change her channel and start listening to people who believed that she could do anything. Soon she believed it as well.

SURROUND YOURSELF WITH YAYSAYERS.

What we need is more Yaysayers, including ourselves – people who will say "Yes!" to us no matter what the idea, the project, or the choice. I don't care if you have to pay someone to say *yes!* to you. Find yourself a Yaysayer. It might be a best friend, your spouse, your therapist, a coach, a networking association, a local community, or a support group like Alcoholics Anonymous. We need to surround ourselves with people who believe in us, who will cheer us on when we are our own Naysayer.

A few years ago, I learned the art of being a Yaysayer when I crossed paths with a pregnant cow and an anxious farmer. I was on a journey by myself driving through Point Reyes National Park north of San Francisco. On the only road through the park, I saw a pregnant cow lying on its side starting to give birth, but obviously struggling. Overjoyed at the serendipity, I stopped my car and watched as the baby calf's feet started coming out and then stopped. I realized the mother cow needed help. Being the only witness, I drove to the nearby farmhouse and alerted the farmer. Instantly concerned, he followed me with the necessary equipment. By the time we returned to the scene, a few more cars passing on the main road had stopped in curiosity, and a crowd started to gather at the fence. With his tools, the farmer used a crank to pull the baby calf out of the mother. I looked around and a huge crowd of people had assembled to witness the birth of a baby cow. We stared in silence as the calf was born, and we gasped as we realized it wasn't moving. The farmer looked up at the crowd, many of whom were children, and anxiety swept over his face. He couldn't let this calf die right in front of all these families.

The farmer started pushing on the calf's chest in hopes that it would bring air and life into the new baby. The crowd was chillingly quiet, as we held our breath willing the calf to breathe. Our eyes didn't move. It was not looking good, and the farmer looked exhausted. And then out of nowhere, I started cheering – I cheered for the farmer to keep going and for the little guy to start breathing. And suddenly the crowd followed. We were all cheering for the farmer and cheering for the baby, and we didn't stop. Stunned, the farmer worked harder to bring life to the calf. After what seemed like an eternity, the calf coughed and lifted its head. It was alive! The crowd went crazy screaming with joy and applauding in celebration of the new life! As we watched the mother cow start feeding her baby, the farmer walked over to thank me. He said that there were many moments that he was going to give up and declare the baby dead, but then he heard us cheering and because of all of our support, he kept going. As Yaysayers, we literally brought life to that calf.

Nurture your Yaysayers. Thank them for being on your side. In addition, become a Yaysayer for others, so you know what it's like to cheer on someone else. Yaysayers need appreciation to understand the impact they have on you. Make an effort to thank your Yaysayers for cheering for you, especially when *you* don't even feel like cheering for you. Show your appreciation by writing a thank-you card, buying them a gift, or thanking them specifically in person. They will be grateful that you have noticed, and it will encourage them to continue Yaysaying. In fact, your appreciation will likely give them the confidence to consciously be a Yaysayer for other people when otherwise they may have easily stopped yaysaying or, worse yet, slipped into naysaying.

Your Nay-dar.

The more you are focused on your beat-the-alarm goals, your dreams, and your life, the more your radar will be sensitized to detect and repel naysaying. Eventually we stop tolerating it altogether because we operate with intensity and a focus on our beat-the-alarm goals. You will soon spot Naysayers coming and realize that you don't have time to engage in any battles with them. As you encounter naysaying, you will smile kindly and think to yourself, "What a shame that she approaches her life that way." You will instantly recognize the beast as it makes its way into the conversation, and you will change the topic or walk away. You will even find yourself proactively steering clear of Naysayers. When people in your life realize that you will no longer tolerate their naysaying, they will either stop or avoid you altogether, annoyed that their naysaying no longer has an audience. The purging of energy-sucking people from your life will clear the space for Yaysayers. And those Naysayers who want to remain a part of your life will be forced to comply with your new rules.

How to Use This Strategy to Create Moxie.

As you begin your journey to create your own moxie, you will cross paths with many Naysayers. As someone who wants to exude moxie, however, you must listen to Yaysayers. Use your mute button on Naysayers and change the channel to get reception only from Yaysayers. Work to deflect the naysaying that threatens to throw you off your path or even delay your journey. Surround yourself with Yaysayers and become one yourself.

Exercises to Choose Your Channel

- Make a list of your Yaysayers.

- Make a list of more ways and places to find Yaysayers.

- Recruit a Yaysayer by asking someone to be your Yaysayer.

- Thank someone for being your Yaysayer.

- Make a list of your Naysayers.

- Predict a naysaying comment from one of your Naysayers. Now write a response that you can use to deflect the naysaying.

- Practice your response the next time the naysaying occurs.

- Intentionally change the conversation with a friend from one of naysaying to one of yaysaying.

Say Yes First, Figure out the How Later

. . . .

Jumping in without a Plan

"Someday when" is the killer of all great ideas and dreams, and results in a lot of "I wish I would haves" at the end of a lifetime. With a myriad of excuses, circumstances, and good reasons, we allow ourselves to get stuck in "someday" and "how." *Someday* we'll do something when we figure out the *how* to do it. The antithesis of "someday," "how," and "I wish I would have," is saying *Yes!* first and figuring out the *how* later

There are many reasons we don't say *Yes!* first, from not enough time or money to a concern over what others will think. Ultimately, each of these reasons can be traced to a fear of failure. Let's explore the rationale we use when we hang our hat on these reasons. Then let's discover how to start saying *Yes!* in spite of a lack of *how.*

NOT ENOUGH TIME.

When is there enough time to do anything? We are overbooked, over stimulated, overextended, and overdone. We fill our lives with so much busyness, and even if we ever checked everything off of our to-do lists, there are 500 channels ready to suck us in. I love it when people tell me how busy they are, and then they meet a new man or woman and suddenly they have time for dating, sleepovers, morning brunches, and afternoon picnics. How did they possibly squeeze time out of their schedules for that? They made the time because they made the relationship a priority. There is never a perfect time to get married, have a baby, change careers, go on a vacation, take an adventure, or even learn to dance. We are always too busy with the life that we created and stuffed to the seams. But we will run out of time if we wait to find the perfect time to start the things we really want to do. We need to declare something a priority and then work life around it. So, let's be honest and say, "I am not ready to do X, Y, or Z and when I am, I'll find the time to do it."

Lack of time is just an excuse. We think we need to carve out time to figure out the *how* before we get started and because we're so busy in our lives right now, we don't have time to figure out the *how*. We might "someday." The reality is that we never have time to figure out the *how*. When we're ready to jump, we will make the time and figure it out as we go.

Often we put pressure on ourselves to do it all: work, parents, spouse, children, and passions. We struggle to be all things to all people. We tend to go an inch deep and cover a mile wide. What if we covered only an inch wide but went a mile deep? Many of us try to do it all, but we fail to do it all as well and with as much fun as we could if we prioritized a few things at a time. The hidden truth is that we *can* do it all; we just don't need to do it all at the same time. Former Chairman and CEO of GE, Jack Welch, once labeled it "work-life choices" instead of work-life balance. We make choices with our time and the minute we acknowledge that, we can choose to create any balance we want.

There is a story of the professor who filled a jar with big rocks and asked his class if the jar was full. The class said "Yes." He then filled the jar with pebbles and asked if the jar was full. Again, the class said "Yes." He then filled the jar with sand and asked if the jar was full. A little more hesitant, the class again said "Yes." He then added enough water to fill it to the top of the jar and declared that the jar was finally full. The point being that if you don't put the big rocks in first (the priorities), the pebbles, sand, and water (our everyday busyness), will take up all the space leaving no room for the big rocks. This is your life. What is important to you? Schedule those things first. Then deal with the to-do lists.

Sometimes we argue that we are too old and therefore don't have enough time left in our life to do something we want to do. These thoughts include, "I'm too old to start working on that. I should have done something years ago when I was young and had more energy." Time is going to continue passing, and you have a choice to do something or not. Jane had always wanted to become a doctor, but she never pursued it because it required eight years of school. Those eight years were going to pass her by whether she went to medical school or not. She finally enrolled at the age of 39.

Age is irrelevant in the pursuit of goals. Individuals like Clara Barton aren't stopped by their age. Clara Barton had been a schoolteacher for two decades when the Civil War broke out in 1861. Moved to make a difference, she left teaching at the age of 40 to distribute food and supplies to soldiers during the war. Even after the war ended she continued her work, and, at age 61, she founded the American Red Cross. When you discover a passion or declare beat-the-alarm goals, as Dr. Jane and Clara Barton did, it is never too late to pursue them.

MONEY.

Everyone talks about how they don't have enough money. Sometimes we really do have enough money to support us, but the mere thought of risking any of it paralyzes us from pursuing our beat-the-alarm goals. No matter how much we have, we complain: "I can't afford it" or "I have no money." But literally speaking, a person with "no money" is someone who has no money in his bank account, no money in his pocket, no change at home, and no access to cash or credit. He lives on the street and is asking for a quarter to buy some food. It's all relative. We spend money in ways that people who really do not have any money find luxurious. We shop like no other country. We spend around $300 million on clothes each day; we spend approximately $8 billion on plastic surgery each year. How much do you spend a day on coffee, food, manicures, clothes, hair products, gasoline, cigarettes, or alcohol? We pay $4 for a cup of coffee with a credit card while complaining about how we can't afford to pursue our dream. Isn't it true that when you really want something you find a way to pay for it? So, essentially not enough money is just an excuse – an excuse not to do something. Be honest and say, "I'm not ready to do X, Y, or Z, and when I am, I will prioritize finding the money to do it."

Concern Over What Other People Will Think.

We spend our whole life worrying what other people will think. Do they like me, do they like my choices, what do they think of me, are they talking about me? It's exhausting trying to get everyone else to like us. Everyone passes judgment on everyone else; we have opinions on how even our closest loved ones live their lives. Often our family, friends, and society put pressure on us to be a certain person or to follow a certain path. It will take moxie to move forward in spite of those pressures and break from their demands and expectations. Someday when we are dead, these countless opinions of others will no longer matter. So, why do we let them run our lives while we are breathing?

Charlene is 48, single, and has never been married. She started dating a man who got divorced after 38 years of marriage to the same woman. When asked why they divorced he said that they were never in love. They got pregnant at 18 and married immediately, but they were never in love. They were in a comfortable existence with friends and family who relied on their staying a married couple. The divorced man then questioned

Charlene about what was wrong with her that she never got married. "Isn't that interesting," she said. "I stay single because I have never found the right guy for me, and society says there's something wrong with my choices. You stay in a loveless marriage wasting away your years and hers, and society says that that is acceptable." There are things we do out of fear of other people's opinions, and staying married to the wrong person often makes it to the top of the list.

It is hard enough to like ourselves, let alone to get everyone else to like us. If we got to the end of our life and could declare that we like ourselves and our own choices, we could say we won. Ever notice that when you finally decide to do something and declare it with conviction – whether it's change jobs, go back to school, get married, have a baby – you move forward in the face of everyone's judgments? (And if you think they are not judging you, you are kidding yourself.) Taking any action will cause the people in your life to express their opinions. Some people will be inspired; some people will cheer you on; some people will be pissed off. All these years we hesitate taking major leaps in our lives for fear of what other people might think of us. In reality, they are going to think whatever they think and they are often going to do whatever they choose in spite of your opinions. Recall that when they disapprove of our actions they could just be upset that they are not as brave as we are to do something new and exciting. Our concern with what others think of us is just an excuse we cling to instead of taking action.

In the face of the opinions and judgments of an entire fan base, Michael Jordan reinvented himself after retiring as one of the greatest basketball players of all time. He declared shortly after retiring that he was going to follow his dream of playing baseball. But the world loved him in his role as the "greatest basketball player" of all time, and they found it hard to see him as a baseball player. Everywhere people expressed their skepticism about his decision. It was hard for people to understand why he would want to try something new after dominating one sport already. And when he ultimately retired from baseball, people declared his career a failure. Despite these high expectations, told-you-so judgments, and lack of full support from his fans, Jordan went forward with his beat-the-alarm goal. That's moxie.

FEAR OF FAILURE.

Isn't the fear of failure what we're really talking about with all of these reasons and excuses for not taking action? Why are we so afraid to fail? What does it mean about us when we try something and fail? It's as if we're afraid we will melt if we fail. At 5 years old this fear did not run our lives. When we were 5, trying new things was a part of growing up. We tried new things because we were learning about life and trying to stand, ride a bike, talk, read, write, and dress ourselves. In fact, if children don't learn to ride a bike at fearless 5, they have a harder time learning as an older child because as they get older, they better comprehend the risk of falling and the harm that may result when they fall. As adults, that risk gets exaggerated in our minds as the fall to the ground seems further and further away. Even though we too are still growing up and learning about life, we fear the fall more now than as children.

Let's look at a few people who have succeeded in spite of their failures. Award-winning actor Humphrey Bogart was once accepted to Yale but never made it due to being expelled from high school for bad behavior shortly before graduation. Oscar-winning filmmaker Oliver Stone failed his second semester college classes choosing instead to work on a book that publishers subsequently rejected. He dropped out of college and moved to Vietnam to teach English and later fight in the Vietnam War. Steve Jobs, CEO of Apple Computers, was once fired by Apple, the same company he helped to create and now leads with great success. All of these people failed but weren't stopped by those failures. They tried something new even though they didn't know how, and when the world rejected them, they didn't stop. They learned from their experience and tried a different approach. They discovered the "how to succeed" on the journey, not before they even started. They didn't wait to figure it out first. That's moxie.

We are all a work in progress. Everyone will know when we are done learning because they will be at our funeral. In the meantime, we are all just navigating our own path. When you discover that you have made a wrong choice or you fail in your attempt to do something new, understand that you are merely in the middle of learning one of those ride-a-bike lessons. When you see others in your life make wrong choices and stumble on their journey, have compassion and know that they too are just learning to ride a bike. The true test of your character and theirs will be what you each do next after the fall.

My grandfather was an alcoholic for many years. My grandmother, a Ma Bell telephone operator, raised their four children often all by herself while my grandfather spent the family's income at the local bar, sometimes disappearing for days on end. When his first grandchild was born, my grandfather joined Alcoholics Anonymous and became sober. He then took on his life. He began cycling and completed a 100-mile bike ride, a beat-the-alarm goal for him. After retirement, he went back to school and earned a degree in counseling and became a counselor for others dealing with alcoholism. He also volunteered as a crossing guard at a local school and helped children get to and from school safely. With his long white beard, thick white hair, big nose, rolling belly and hearty laugh, he also volunteered as Santa Claus during each Christmas holiday. By the time he passed away he was 38 years sober, happily married to my grandmother for over 60 years, had enjoyed five doting grandchildren and four great-grandchildren, had a lifetime of experiences and lessons, and left a town full of adoring fans. Was he a failure or a success? Guess it depends on when you judge him.

There is a saying, "What would you do if you knew you could not fail?" Instead ask yourself "What are you *not* doing because you are afraid of failing?" What is paralyzing you? What are you afraid to do? What are you putting off until someday with a slew of excuses around time, money, or other concerns?

THE HOW.

The ubiquitous *how*. How will we pay for it? How will we make the time? How will it work out? How will we handle it if it doesn't work out? How will we stomach the failure? How will we deal with other people who are judging us? We can spend so much time trying to figure out the *how* that it paralyzes us, and we don't move at all.

The problem with figuring out the *how* before we even begin is that even if we do figure it out, inevitably the *how* will not go as planned. Rarely does anything go as planned. When was the last time something went exactly as you planned? It's frustrating when life does not go according to our plans, and this frustration sometimes stops us from taking any further action. When we aren't stopped, we figure out the *how* while we are in the midst of the doing. So, we need to ask, if life never turns out as we plan and we actually discover how to do things when we jump in and do them, then why do we spend so much time figuring out the *how*?

Watch television and you'll see that this figuring-out-the-how-as-we-go approach actually entertains us when it's not our own life. In sitcoms in particular, when the main characters share their plans with the audience about how they are going to solve their particular crisis, notice that their pre-crafted solutions never turn out as the main characters had planned. In the midst of taking action, the main characters discover their plan didn't work because of something they hadn't thought of, and so they are forced to find another way. On TV this is entertaining; in our lives we aren't so entertained. What if we were? What if we approached our lives as an adventure?

When we choose to figure out the *how* as we go, we are guaranteed to experience adventure and excitement. When we get stopped by the *how*, we don't take action, and we are guaranteed to continue the life we have. I know one desperate housewife who complains to her husband endlessly, "This is not the life I signed up for!" Her mantra will continue until she comprehends that her reality is the result of her own choices and her own fear of the unknown. When you say you didn't sign up for this life and then you don't make any changes, often for fear of the *how*, you just signed up for that life.

Learning to say *Yes!* to adventures, opportunities, dreams, and our life requires us to shift our focus from our fears to our goals. A few tactics help us make this shift: asking "what's the worst that could happen?," pretending that money's no object, engaging our Yaysayers, planning less, practicing, and being ourselves. All of these tactics fuel LifeMoxie! Strategy #4.

What's the Worst That Could Happen?

As kids, whenever we hesitated out of fear, my mom would say, "What's the worst that could happen?" As if a game had just been presented, we would explore all the possible things that could happen as a result of trying something new. After considering each scenario, we would determine that we could survive any of them — good, bad, and ugly — so we would move forward and give whatever it was a try. This gave us the freedom and confidence to fly! It is with that same what's-the-worst-that-can-happen attitude that I moved across country after law school, taught 12-year-old girls about business, and quit my last job to pursue LifeMoxie! It is with this what's-the-worst-that-can-happen mantra that entrepreneurs start businesses, politicians run for office, people experience adventures, and you can take on your life.

My crazy friend Robin, a master at what's-the-worst-that-can-happen, once joined the circus with this mantra. She first entertained the idea of being a trapeze artist while visiting Club Med in the Bahamas with her parents and taking a public lesson at the resort circus. Upon returning home and splitting with her boyfriend, she longed to go back. Robin and a friend returned to Club Med over college spring break; this time she headed right for the circus tent. With moxie in tow, she spent time with the trapeze team until they gave her the opportunity to audition for the team and offered her a job in the circus. In a moxie moment, she decided to stay. Robin said *Yes!* without knowing the *how* – how she was going to support herself, finish college, or deal with the life she left behind. She determined that in the worst case she'd hate it and move back home with a new life experience in her pocket. Robin was more committed to the adventure than she was about others' judgments and opinions about her. Robin spent two years in the circus and returned home to finish college and then go on to law school and business school. To this day there is a sparkle in her eyes when she recounts this adventure, evidencing the priceless experience that what's-the-worst-that-can-happen gifted her.

When I discovered the entrepreneurial program at an all-girls middle school, I rediscovered a passion that had me ask what's-the-worst-that-can-happen. When the opportunity to be a co-director of the program opened up I instantly said *Yes!*, having no clue how I was going to run the program while managing my other job running the legal department of a public company. I thought about the worst that could happen and could only imagine that I would have to work longer hours to fulfill both responsibilities. I felt that passing up this opportunity would actually be the worst that could happen. It also occurred to me that I knew nothing about pre-adolescent girls, teaching, entrepreneurship, or running an educational program. Again, I didn't want to pass up this experience so I said *Yes!* determined to figure out the *how* as I went. Everything after that became an adventure and my own priceless exprience.

Money's No Object.

Growing up, my mom also fed us the "money's no object" mantra. This is both freedom-giving and dangerous. Freedom-giving because it eliminates one of the main excuses for why we don't take action: money. Dangerous because it has the potential of encouraging a world void of reality. Without LifeMoxie! Strategy #1 – a clear picture of where you're headed – the money's-no-object mantra can quickly become the object itself. Unless you are operating from clear missions and beat-the-alarm goals, it is easy to get lost in the fantasy that money really is no object.

As we explored earlier in this chapter, money is often an objection that people raise for not doing something they really want to do; they just can't afford it or they are too concerned about risking the money they do have. Whenever we harbored a dream as kids, my mom would sing, "Money's no object!" (even though growing up on a farm skimping and saving we knew it really was). If money even came up as a concern, my mom would interrupt with, "What if money was no object?" This allowed us to explore other ways to either obtain the money or do what we wanted to do, go where we wanted to go, and experience all we wanted, in spite of the lack of money. It was because of this "money's no object" attitude that I was not stopped from going to law school based on my lack of money to pay for it. Being determined to go, I quickly discovered an entire world of school loans established just for people like me. I did not hesitate to borrow the money and was rewarded with my greatest academic experience.

Entrepreneurs similarly must be willing to put the money objection in perspective if they are to succeed. The business world is brimming with individuals who have risked their life savings for the chance of making it big with their ideas. They embrace the "money's no object" mantra to allow themselves to focus on their beat-the-alarm goal. The entrepreneurs who are not ready to take a risk use money as the objection for not moving forward. They are more concerned about what they will lose in the short term and want more of a guarantee of future success before they jump in. These entrepreneurs are still trying to figure out the *how*.

When I was dancing with the idea of quitting my job to start my own business, the money was a huge obstacle for me as well. I had a mortgage to pay all by myself not to mention a lifestyle that I had grown accustomed to. I learned that a friend landed a position with a temp agency making $25 an hour, which equated to about $50,000 a year. I could do that, I thought, and I could live on that. Suddenly the-worst-that-could-happen objection – I fail and need to get a job – and the money objection were instantly handled. The door to my adventure was no longer locked. What door in your life is locked as a result of fear over money? What if money was not an object, what would you do?

Tell It to a Yaysayer.

If you're ready to say *Yes!* first before figuring out the *how*, tell it to a Yaysayer. Whatever doubts may be springing from your tongue, their encouragement will help you swallow them before they reach oxygen. Yaysayers assure us that whatever needs to be figured out, will be. If you are learning to shout *Yes!* to your ideas and dreams, be sure to say it first to a Yaysayer.

Patty started her business by doing just that – she said *Yes!* first and then immediately called her Yaysayer. She wanted to open her own hand-therapy practice. For months she was stuck in a state of how, pregnant with circumstances, excuses, and somedays. And then one day, she called LifeMoxie! to report that she had signed a lease for an office and asked if we could help her with whatever she needed to do next. Stunned with admiration for her moxie, we got to work. Patty didn't wait to figure it all out; she jumped, and three years later her practice continues to thrive giving her self-respect, independence, confidence, and cash flow. She often shares with us that had she stopped to figure out all that was involved in starting her own practice, she doesn't think she would have ever taken the first step. Because Patty jumped, she didn't have time to over-plan, analyze, or figure it all out. She just made time to call her Yaysayer.

STOP OVER-PLANNING.

We spend so much time planning that someone actually coined the term "paralysis by analysis." Our minds race as we plan every aspect of a situation: what will we say, what will we do, what will we do if it doesn't work? Some planning is essential, but too much planning keeps us perpetually frozen.

The business plan is one of those things that can cause us to spend too much time in the *how* and not enough time in the doing. We think that we need to have it all figured out before we start the business, and yet we learn the most about our business when we actually dive in and start doing, like Patty did with her hand-therapy practice. Inevitably we will discover things about our business model, our product, or the market that we hadn't thought about when we did our planning. The best approach is to treat your business plan like your life plan – you'll never be done working on it. You will continue to tweak, update, and revise it while you are in the process of running your business. So, write the plan while you make the product or test the service, and learn as you go. Keep the business plan with you at all times as you launch and let it act as a repository for your learnings. After the first few years of carrying around your plan, commit to updating your business plan every three to six months based on the learnings you acquire from running your business and stay committed to figuring it out in the process.

Every year the teams in the entrepreneurial education program at the all-girls school learn the lesson of the never-completed business plan. One year a team set out to produce and sell "sweet-smelling pillows." To achieve the sweet smell, they added lavender to each pillow before sewing them shut. What they didn't plan for but quickly discovered is that lavender rots over time. Soon they had rotting inventory and unhappy customers. Going back to the business plan they exchanged the lavender for lavender drops. While they were able to achieve the sweet smell in their pillows, they found a way to do it using different materials than originally planned. The entrepreneurial program gives the girls permission to jump in and figure it all out as they go.

Our life plans work the same way. We can do some planning, but it's only when we get out there and live that we learn about our life. I am often amused by the new parents who plan out their child's life on the way home from the hospital and for years to follow. They declare that she is not going to eat any sugar; she will only wear pink and play with Barbie; she will go to private school; she will take piano lessons and tap dance; she will attend college and travel abroad for a year; and she will be a Republican like her dad and a doctor like her mom. Life doesn't work this way; life works by living it. So, while her parents are busy planning her life, she's busy living it.

In 1984 Madonna had just released her *Like a Virgin* album. To some she was offensive; to others she was strange; to many she was inspiring. Her unmatched, ripped clothes and lace midriff-outfits flew in the face of fashion norms. Her edgy and provocative music incensed critics. Her evasive, sexy, and aloof performances pushed all boundaries in the music industry. And girls everywhere began to emulate her style. When Dick Clark interviewed her on national television during her debut on *American Band Stand,* he asked her what she wanted to do with her life. Without blinking an eye, she looked right into the camera and said, "I'm going to rule the world." Note she did not say "I hope to rule the world," or "I'm going to try to figure out a way to rule the world," or "I am currently in the process of drafting a detailed plan to rule the world." Instead she declared it with such conviction that we had no other choice but to believe her. In 1984 Madonna had no idea how she was going to rule the world or even what that meant. She didn't have it all figured out. But she didn't wait to plan it all out either. She just declared what she wanted and ran in that direction. Twenty years later, she has done just that. Madonna has ventured into music, modeling, dancing, singing, movies, theater, writing books (from X-rated to children's), and motherhood. For years she ruled the music world, and 20 years later she continues to rule her own world.

Madonna is a role model for saying *Yes!* first. She is constantly reinventing herself. She takes on projects that are aligned with her missions. She takes risks. She has adventures. She is resourceful. She is up for a challenge. She has failed more than once. But Madonna has never been stopped for lack of a plan.

More Spit Less Shine.

If we would just be ourselves. We saw earlier that our concern over what other people will think often prevents us from saying *Yes!* first and figuring out the how later. As a result of worrying so much what others think, we sacrifice being ourselves. We are taught at a young age to please others and to hunger for their approval. "Be a good girl." "Be a good boy." From our parents, to our teachers, to our employers, we spend our whole life trying to be something for someone else. As a result, we often fail to be ourselves. Even Shakespeare had it right when he philosophized, "To thine own self be true." But it's challenging to be true to yourself when you are so busy pleasing everyone else.

Wouldn't it be great if we didn't care what anyone thought? The reality of human nature is that we'll always be concerned with what some people think of us. The trick is to stay intensely focused on our beat-the-alarm goals that genuinely excite us (not them). The more we keep the focus, the easier it is to be dauntless and stay undeterred by their thoughts, judgments, and opinions. Not intimidated, we will say *Yes!* to opportunities that further those beat-the-alarm goals in the face of what others think. When we are intensely focused on accomplishing beat-the-alarm goals that light us up, we will forget to worry what *they* all think. We'll be too busy enjoying our life. To do what she has done, Madonna has had to master this. Many people love her and her music, while many others despise her, her music, and her lifestyle. Most of us are in some way intrigued by her life. Madonna doesn't seem to care. She operates as if she is oblivious whether you like her or not, even if she does care. Madonna lives her life based on what she wants to accomplish, not what you want her to accomplish. That's moxie.

Erin Brockovich (portrayed by Julia Roberts in the movie of the same name) did not let anyone's judgments faze her in pursuing her beat-the-alarm goal. She became enraged over the harm that the residents of a small town suffered as a result of the local utility company's dumping of waste. Her passion for proving the company's liability and holding them accountable to the community members for their pain and suffering drove Erin forward in spite of others' constant judgments about her. They judged her scanty outfits, her lack of education, her ignorance about the legal process, her brazenness – who did she think she was? – and her inexperience. Erin noticed their looks, their snickers, their laughs, and their raised eyebrows, but she didn't allow it all to faze her. She remained maniacally focused on her beat-the-alarm goal and, as a result, helped win the largest settlement ever paid in a direct action lawsuit in U.S. history.

Consider where you are sacrificing your true self for fear of others' opinions. What would happen if you made a choice that you knew would disappoint or upset someone else but made you happy? As long as you operate from clarified missions and articulated beat-the-alarm goals, your choices may cause upset, judgment, or raised eyebrows, but no one will melt. Now imagine your life 10 years from now. Either you still haven't accomplished your beat-the-alarm goal and you've managed to keep everyone happy, or you have followed your heart, and everyone else found a way to adjust and go on with their lives. Which scenario can you live with?

Bob, a well-respected doctor who loved and cared for his family and the community, was feeling stuck in his life. He wanted to pursue his dream of seeing the world, but he was afraid of what everyone would think of his leaving his practice. He enrolled his family in the support of his beat-the-alarm goal and left for a year-long adventure exploring South America and volunteering with Doctors Without Borders. Many people in town passed judgment – how dare he leave his wife to fend for herself, and why would anyone leave a thriving medical practice such as his? He accomplished his beat-the-alarm goal and returned home with a renewed passion for his life. The town jury with all of their judgments managed to adjust to life in spite of Bob's choices.

It takes practice to remain unfazed in your journey in spite of others' opinions. Sometimes it's easier to make life-changing progress in day-changing steps. When a frog is put into a pot of water on a stove and the heat is slowly turned up, the frog does not notice. When the water eventually comes to a boil, the frog cooks and dies, even though he could have jumped out of the water. He could have saved himself, but he didn't notice that the water was getting hotter. This phenomenon is evidenced in our lives. When we were bright-eyed, bushy-tailed teenagers, we were revolted at the thought that 20 years into the future we would tolerate a miserable job, a flat-lined marriage, an unacceptable situation, or discarded dreams. And yet, it happens one day at a time until the water in our life is boiling, and we don't even realize it.

We can also apply that same approach the other way to make drastic changes to our lives in our favor. If it feels too overwhelming to make sweeping life changes like changing your career or even your mailing address, make little changes in that direction one day at a time. For instance, take a class to study a new profession as you consider it or visit a city you have dreamt about moving to. Sometimes turning up the heat in our own lives a few degrees at a time will make it easier for us to head in a new direction or just start being ourselves.

Incorporating this "say yes" strategy into your life requires that you place a priority on your missions and your beat-the-alarm goals over your concern for others' opinions of you. Test the waters with a few simple moves and see how quickly you stop worrying about others when you're busy being yourself and enjoying your life.

STOP TRYING TO FIGURE IT ALL OUT.

"Stop trying to figure it all out" takes similar muscles and practice as "stop worrying what others will think." Have you ever said *Yes!* to something while having no clue what you were in store for? What did that feel like? You probably figured it out as you went and got to the other side in one piece with a new experience.

There are many ways to build this muscle. Sign up for a class to learn something new, like dancing, foreign language, or cooking. Notice that you are entering the class without knowing how you'll get to the end with new skills. You figure it out as you go.

Another way to practice is to consciously say *Yes!* to any new project at home or at work before asking any questions. Stop yourself from asking how; just say *Yes!* and commit to figuring out the *how* as you go. For example, if your spouse approaches you with a suggestion that the family go on vacation and you instantly think of all the reasons why you shouldn't go – money, time, work, appointments, soccer schedules, birthday parties – say *Yes!* anyway and set a date for the vacation. If your boss approaches you with an idea for a new product, say *Yes!* and pull a research team together to get started immediately. Stop the instant litany of objections before they leave your tongue. Just stomach it and pretend that it will all work out somehow. Fake a smile of enthusiasm if you have to!

Another way to practice is to take the initiative and enroll others in new adventures without having all of the details figured out. For example, enroll your significant other or your team at work into a wacky, off-the-wall idea that clearly furthers a mission but, that from the outset, seems nearly impossible. You could present to them the idea of a week-long bike trip through the Swiss Alps, dance lessons, a department bowling league, or a new web site for the company. When they question your idea and need to know more of the *how*, stop them from diving deep into the process, and ensure them that together you'll have a great experience and learn a lot. (They will likely think you are crazy, so serendipitously you will be practicing the stop-worrying-what-they-think muscle as well.)

According to her high-school boyfriend, Oprah knew at that young age exactly what she wanted to do with her life – her empire was brewing inside her early on. She stayed focused on her beat-the-alarm goals and overall missions rather than others' opinions. She didn't over-plan; she didn't stop long enough to figure it all out. She didn't have time – the ship was leaving, and she jumped on. Oprah created her empire along the way.

From reporting on the weather, to anchoring the news, to taking over a flailing morning talk show in Chicago and directly competing with Phil Donahue, Oprah knows how to jump when opportunities present themselves to her. In 1986 Oprah launched her television talk show. At the time, the market was oversaturated with talk shows – Phil Donahue, Montel Williams, Maury Povich, and Ricki Lake, to name a few. Everyone who was anyone already had a daytime talk show. The last thing we needed was another one. We especially didn't need one from an unknown news anchor. The deck was stacked against her from the beginning. Adding to that tall deck was Oprah's less than fabulous talk show skills. Episodes from 1986 found on her 20th anniversary CD collection released in 2006 evidence how far Oprah has come as the talk show diva. Twenty years prior, her television studio looked dated, her hair and clothes appeared frumpy, and even her interviewing style was unpolished. Her head bounced when she interviewed guests and her eyes jumped frenetically from the camera to the audience to her guest. She was melodramatic, overly serious, and lacked the confidence and swagger we see today. Looking back, she was good, but not great. What she did have, however, was an intense commitment to being the best and curiosity, humor, and empathy that compelled her guests to reveal things on national television as if in group therapy. She used these qualities to create her empire. She didn't wait to figure it all out. Consciously operating from her missions and her beat-the-alarm goals, she says *Yes!* without figuring it all out first. That's moxie.

Like Oprah, Jim Carrey was once an unknown with big dreams. He wanted to become a famous actor. As a show of commitment to his success, he wrote himself a $10 million check at the launch of his career. He carried this with him until the day he was able to cash it. He had no idea how he was going to cash that check, but he drove in that direction, maniacal about his career and his dreams. Jim Carrey did not wait to figure it all out; he said *Yes!* first. Like all thriving actors, musicians, and entrepreneurs, Jim Carrey became bigger than life by taking actions first and then figuring out the *how* of his dreams as he stumbled down the path of his journey.

We look at musicians, actors, and other rich and famous people with stars in our eyes. We're in awe of their success, we marvel at their popularity and wealth, and we wonder how they got to be so darn lucky. But Oprah, Madonna, Bruce Springsteen, the Beatles, Microsoft founder Bill Gates, and Lance Armstrong didn't wake up one morning with an empire at their feet. They started where you're starting: with an idea, a passion, a dream. They employed all nine strategies in some way to create their own moxie from which they built their empires. Blaming it all on their luck, we lose sight of the hard work and moxie they employed to get where they are. Luck is being prepared when opportunity knocks; but moxie is being prepared and then making opportunity knock.

How to Use This Strategy to Create Moxie.

Revisit your missions and your beat-the-alarm goals. What if you said *Yes!* to one of your beat-the-alarm goals without any idea how to make it happen? First of all, put the money concerns aside for a moment. Then ask yourself what is the worst that can happen. Consider that failure is merely a fall off the bike. Make a list of all of your objections. Make a list of other people's objections. Are these objections founded or is there some fear underlying them? In the face of those fears, what if you declared that you were going to pursue that beat-the-alarm goal anyway? Give up the *how* and get ready to soar!

Exercises to Say Yes First, Figure out the How Later

- Make a list of reasons that cause you to hesitate from saying *Yes!* first.

- Describe something that you would do if only you knew how.

- Describe something that you would do if you knew you wouldn't fail.

- Describe something that you would do if only money was not standing in the way.

- Think of a time that you did something without knowing how to do it. How did it turn out?

Act As If

. . . .
Fakin' It 'Til You Make It

'Act *as if* is at the core of having moxie. It means fake it 'til you make it. It's the attitude that creates the courage you need to say *Yes!* first, to ask, to be uncomfortable, and to live with boldness, and to keep moving. It provides ammunition when the Naysayers attack, including the ones in your head. Act as if and get ready for your moxie to open doors of opportunity.

Fake It 'Til You Make It.

When you act as if, you are fakin' it 'til you make it. This attitude instills confidence in your audience that you are the right person to do the job, meanwhile buying you the time to figure out how to do that job. For example, if you act as if you are the perfect person to lead the basketball team to championship, you will open the door of opportunity and force your foot in. You now have a fighting chance to be chosen as the coach. If instead you approach the opportunity with uncertainty, insecurity, and timidity, the door will never open for you, and if it does, it will likely slam shut on your foot. Why not go into situations with an air of "I can do this," and "I am the right person," and at least open the door? To even have the chance to prove yourself, you need doors to open, and fakin' it 'til you make it is a door-opener that will buy you time to actually make it.

Many negotiating experts claim that men negotiate higher starting salaries than women because men flaunt an I-can-do-this-job-with-my-eyes-closed attitude during interviews. They act as if they already possess the skills needed to be a wild success at the job for which they are interviewing. They act as if the employer would be lucky to get them. They don't act as if they must prove themselves first. Women, on the other hand, generally feel the necessity to prove themselves first. Women hedge their bets when discussing their ability to succeed at a job, usually because they don't want to over promise and then disappoint. When a woman is not feeling 100 percent confident she will be successful, she sets an employer's expectations low, accepts a lower salary, and then works her butt off in hopes that her employer will notice and reward her with a raise for her hard work. This approach gambles time and money, for there is no guarantee an employer will ever recognize hard work, how long it may take for such recognition, and what money, if any, will be rewarded for it. Conversely, if she acts *as if* at the beginning, she could be rewarded with the title and the money first and then be granted the opportunity to prove herself.

The business reality show *The Apprentice* attracts contestants who must also fake it 'til they make it. The show's host, Donald Trump wants winners on his team, not losers. He wants people to act as if they already have the job. In fact, he uses this forum to ascertain how these individuals will act on his team in the real world, so he provides them with real-life situations in which to test them. As a result, the people who apply to *The Apprentice* act *as if* in order to survive from week to week. This approach buys them time to figure out what needs to be done to succeed in a project before Trump yells, "You're fired!" The contestants who eventually make it to the end have successfully communicated with confidence, conviction, certainty, and passion, regardless of how they may have felt on the inside along the way.

I learned the power of acting *as if* when I launched the corporate division at LifeMoxie! I quickly discovered that our target client, large corporations, rarely like to be the guinea pig. They want to hire vendors who have been-there-done-that and can flaunt proven programs, a track record, results, and a marked return on investment with other corporations. We had none of that. All we had was a conviction that our idea for mentoring was a solution the corporate world was missing. We had absolutely no experience with any company, and I was unclear how we were going to accomplish this vision. While the say-yes-first-figure-out-the-how-later attitude got us this far, I needed something else to get a *Yes!* from our first corporation. I needed to act as if we were the solution they needed to fix their professional development challenges, even if I had my internal doubts and insecurities. I met a woman at a conference who wanted to bring a mentoring program to her company. Acting *as if* I had the solution she was looking for (in spite of the fact that it remained a figment of my imagination and even at that uncertain), I shared with her our approach to mentoring, and I did so with conviction, passion, and an act-as-if attitude. She was hooked. She invited me to participate in a dog and pony show with other vendors pitching their solutions to the company, and again my act-as-if attitude won the day. We landed our first contract, which launched our corporate solutions division. The next day we went to work figuring out how we were going to actually deliver what we just promised.

Carrie also discovered the power of acting *as if* when she declared herself an expert. As an art fanatic, she is passionate about teaching people to love art. She also harbored a beat-the-alarm goal to work at the Guggenheim in New York doing just that. Unfortunately, all of the art museums in the city refused to entertain her passion because she did not hold a PhD. Carrie and

I decided that the PhD merely indicated a level of expertise, and that if she went back to school, she would be earning a degree so that someone else could declare that she had a level of expertise. We decided that she should skip the PhD program and instead focus on creating and declaring her own expertise immediately. She found a niche that excited her – the looting of art – and we just declared that she possessed expertise in the looting of art. In fact, we started calling her the expert in our first meeting. Why wait? Who was going to point a finger and say, "Hey Carrie! You're not an expert!" No one. So we printed business cards that dubbed her the expert in the looting of art. She went on to write a book, hone her expertise in the process, deliver speeches, and develop programs on her expertise. Soon the Guggenheim demanded that Carrie share her expertise with their patrons during weekly programs. Carrie became an expert the instant she declared it and started acting *as if*.

BATTLING THE NAYSAYERS.

You may be full of passion and conviction that you want to change your life, take an adventure, start a business, or find a new career, but others are going to be doubtful at first, especially your Naysayers. Projecting an act-as-if attitude that says "I'm already succeeding" will cause people to believe you and doubt their own instinctual judgment that you will fail. People just want to be right, and if you are selling a better story than they have made up about you, then they are going to start believing you. Remember we are constantly battling the Naysayers, including the ones in our head. By taking on this act-as-if attitude, we are projecting the confidence – even if manufactured – that will suspend others' naysaying long enough to give us the chance to prove ourselves.

Acting as if also allows us to battle our biggest Naysayer – ourselves. We are our biggest self-doubter. When we act *as if*, we start diluting the power of our self-doubt. It is important that we step into who we really want to be in order to start tasting success, fueling our confidence, and creating a desire for more of it. The more we start acting *as if*, the more we will start believing in ourselves.

The Program Director for the teen program at LifeMoxie! landed her coveted position in spite of the Naysayers in her head. Mikki came to her first meeting armed with a deep passion for empowering teens but fraught with self-doubt. She dreamt of working with teens coaching them to feel powerful, but like all of us at one time or another, she battled her low self-confidence. She knew she would need to act *as if* in order to get our attention as someone we needed on our team. She worked hard to act as the person that she wanted to be so that we didn't see that she was really just a bundle of insecurities. As a result, we saw her as the person with the expertise and passion that we badly needed. So we hired her. Mikki's internal naysaying didn't stand a chance against the newfound confidence created by her acting *as if*. She soon came to believe what she projected and went on to lead the program with leadership, vision, and confidence.

Open Doors.

When you act *as if*, people believe as if. Doors of opportunity will fly open; and when they do, start walking through with your head held high even if you're shaking in your patent leathers. Acting *as if* is the secret weapon of successful entrepreneurs, successful sales people, and successful job candidates. Acting as if can even open doors personally. What woman wouldn't want to go on a date with a guy who acted *as if* he were going to hand her happily ever after?

Many a door has been opened in Silicon Valley, the land of ideas and money because wide-eyed entrepreneurs acted *as if*. Every day in Silicon Valley, venture capitalists (VCs), the investors who fund start-up companies, support ideas with financial backing. In doing so, they are betting that an idea will be the next Google or Amazon.com, and they want in on the action at the beginning. The energy that drives Silicon Valley is the fear VCs harbor that they might miss out on the next great idea. And how do VCs know when a great idea has been presented to them? Sometimes it's their years of experience in investing in ideas that tells them; sometimes it's a study of the market that gives such an indication; more often than not it's because the founder of the idea acts as if it's the greatest idea since sliced bread.

People complain that most of the companies being funded by venture capitalists in Silicon Valley are founded by men. Having worked in the Valley for 12 years as a corporate attorney and now understanding how important acting *as if* is, it is not surprising that more women-founded companies are not funded by venture capital money. Just like when they interview for jobs, women generally want to accomplish something first to show that they can do it before they start bragging about it. Women typically do not like to toot their own horn without having mastered the toot behind the horn. Unfortunately for women, acting *as if* is crucial to closing any kind of financing in the Valley. What VC wants to invest money in a "well, it might work, but I'm not sure" founder? If women want to get in on the money thrown around in the Valley, they need to start acting as if their ideas are the next big thing to hit the street — even if they aren't, even if they have their own doubts about their ideas or their own ability to succeed. If women want to start playing with the big boys, they need to start acting *as if*, like the big boys do. That would be moxie.

In the height of the dot.com bubble, one of my clients at the law firm sold a successful business on an idea that never made it off the paper on which it was written. His idea was like every other idea in Silicon Valley — it was going to make him and the investors millions. But unlike most other start-ups in the Valley, he didn't have a prototype. He didn't even know if his idea could work. But he was a master at acting *as if*. He sold his idea to a group of VCs for an initial investment of $5 million. As the company grew in employees he still didn't have the product done, but he convinced the investors to invest an additional $13 million into his business. A year and a half went by and still no product to show. He then sold the entire company to a large public company for $300 million. Other than ideas on paper, there was not much evidence of his efforts. What he did have was a lot of moxie. He acted *as if* and as a result the investors were sure they were going to be missing out on something huge if they didn't jump in and play. They jumped and, in the end, they were all rewarded nicely.

Successful sales people know that they need to open doors in order to make a sale, so they master the art of acting *as if* in order to open those doors. And because men are great at acting "*as if*," they are more prevalent in sales careers than women. They have no qualms about convincing others that a product or service will solve all of their problems, even before they know it's true. Men act as if the product or service they are selling is as great as the Internet. They aren't lying. It's not about men's ability to lie. It's about their ability to project confidence about themselves and their solutions first, and then prove themselves second. Whereas women feel they need to prove themselves first in order to feel the confidence they need to project. This is often their sales handicap.

How to Act as If.

The Wizard in the movie *The Wizard of Oz* mastered the *act as if*. No one questioned the Wizard's authority, his power, or his command of the throne. The all-powerful Wizard, as he came to be known, caused people to shudder in his presence. He used threatening and frightful words; his voice boomed; his large head and demaniacal face instilled fear; the smoke and dark green curtain gave an aura of mystery; the big chilling castle, the guards, and his demand to kill the Wicked Witch of the West all screamed power and royalty. He used these tools to act as if he were the supreme ruler of the land; as a result, everyone believed he was the great and almighty Wizard who ruled the Land of Oz. And so he was.

The Scarecrow, the Lion, and the Tin Man, on the other hand, each disempowered themselves with their attitude, and so their words, their voice, their actions, and their body language followed. The Scarecrow did not believe he had any brains, and so he did not act as if he did. The Lion did not believe that he had any courage, and so he did not act as if he did. And the Tin Man did not believe that he had any heart, and so he did not act as if he did. Through their journey down the yellow brick road, they each discovered that their power was inside them all along. They did not need the Wizard to grant them brains, courage, and heart; they just needed to start acting as if they had them. Once they realized that their actions fed their beliefs, and that those beliefs fed their actions, they were able to declare themselves smart, courageous, and full of heart.

Your Words.

Our words can exalt or bury us. Notice when people coat their sentences with "This may sound stupid, but..." or "I'm not sure this is a good idea, but..." They are telling us that what is about to come out of their mouth is stupid and not a very good idea before we have a chance to decide for ourselves. They have caused us to discount their contribution, and they haven't even contributed anything yet.

Space-fillers such as "You know" and "You know what I mean" have a similar effect. I have a friend who starts and ends every sentence with "You know what I mean" and when I'm lucky there is a "You know what I mean" in between pauses within her sentence. It is highly distracting and makes it extremely difficult to focus on what she is saying. People begin using these phrases to fill dead air and buy time to formulate their next thought, and soon they become habitual. Let's bring back the silence and dump the "You knows." These words instantly detract from our credibility and chip away at our confidence.

Acting "as if" requires that our words shout self-confidence and self-assuredness regardless of how we feel inside. We aren't lying; we are acting as if we have that confidence and assuredness already. Successful sales people, entrepreneurs, and job candidates don't lie; they choose words that show confidence in their ability to successfully provide a great solution, launch a great company, or perform great work on the job.

Words either contribute to or contaminate our ability to act *as if*. Words that contaminate include "I'm not sure," "I'm not confident," "I hope to," "I'm going to try to," "I think we can," "Probably," and "I'd like to." For example, "I'm going to try to be there." In other words, you're saying, "I'll certainly give it my all, but I may be a victim to a million other circumstances, including my own feelings, in which case I won't be there." Talk about a lack of commitment. Instead, choose words that give the listener *and* you confidence in you, your ability, and your commitment. Words that contribute to our act-as-if attitude include, "I am confident," "You will not be disappointed," and "I will succeed." Wouldn't you rather buy from someone, give money to someone's business, or hire the person who says, "I'm going to succeed!"? Again, it's not lying, it's saying "I am committed to succeeding, and I will do just that. I may not be 100 percent sure how that will happen, but I will make it happen."

Your Voice.

It's not always what you say; it's how you say it. While we know that what you say does impact your ability to act *as if*, how you say it is equally important. The tone, the volume, the pace, the inflection all contribute to or contaminate the listener's confidence and your own. A weak tone makes your words weak. Being soft-spoken reflects timidity and insecurity. Speak up! If you speak all of your sentences with a really high-pitched voice, it deteriorates your message because you will sound as if you are 7 years old. If you speak all of your sentences with a deep tenor voice, you instill unnecessary fear in your audiences. If you are "uptailing" the ends of your sentences, you start sounding like you are asking a series of questions instead of making confident statements. Notice how your voice impacts the delivery of your statements and ultimately how you and your audience feel about you.

As part of the entrepreneurial program at the all-girls school, the 12-year-old girls were required to present their business plans to an audience of 400 people. The fear and lack of confidence they felt inside echoed in the inflection of their voices during practice. While they read from their notes and PowerPoint slides, they ended each sentence with an uptail, as if they were questioning their own words. We worked for weeks training them to end their sentences with confidence, forcing their voices to head down at the end instead of up. Instantly they sounded more confident and self-assured, even if they were shaking in their skin. This allowed the girls to walk on stage and start feeling as confident as they acted.

Often professional speakers hire singing teachers to help them create variety with their voice. Our vocal chords need exercise just like our muscles. If we spend most of our time speaking with a high-pitched, mousy voice, we need practice changing the pitch to include more convincing, self-assured tenor tones. Start singing in the shower and notice the variety of tones that are required by music. This variety is similarly required to speak with confidence. Record yourself and study your voice. Before sending a voice mail message to someone, replay your message and notice how the tone of your voice imparts an emotion. Notice if you speak too quickly or too slowly, if you are too loud or too soft, if your pitch is too high or too low, and if you uptail your sentences. Notice if you feel confident in you based only on listening to your own voice. Now listen to a recording of a professional speaker. What do they do with their voice that evokes confidence? Play it again and then pause the recording after each sentence. Repeat the sentence and parrot their tone and inflection. This is great practice for creating variety in your voice and, ultimately, confidence in yourself and your audience.

YOUR BODY LANGUAGE.

Dr. Albert Mehrahian, a professor at UCLA, concluded in a research study that our understanding of another person's communication is determined 7 percent by words, 38 percent by tone of voice, and 55 percent by body language. Each of these factors determine the trust and confidence we feel in another person. That means that 93 percent of our communication is at risk if our voice and body language do not align with our words. Conversely, this also means that we have the opportunity to influence 93 percent of our communication with only a few tweaks to our body language or our voice.

Your eyes may be the windows to your soul, but your body language is the window to your confidence. How we hold our head, our hands, our shoulders, and our feet all mirror how we feel inside. If you tilt your head, it says you are not sure of what you are saying; if you wring your hands, it says you are nervous; if you slump your shoulders, it says you are trying to shrink so as not to be noticed; if you stand with your feet pointed inwards, it says you are weak and unsure. Even nervous tics taint another's confidence in our words. Biting fingernails, twirling hair, swaying back and forth, picking scabs, and laughing inappropriately are all indications that you are not self-assured. When we don't project confidence, we don't feel confident in us and consequently, other people don't feel confidence in us.

A FedEx commercial underscores the power of body language, voice, and words on our communication. A group of white-shirted men are sitting in a company meeting brainstorming how to save money. One man says with a tilt of his head, a soft voice, a questioning inflection, an apologetic expression, and slumped shoulders, "Excuse me? I have an idea? Well, maybe if we went with FedEx we could save money by using their ground service that gives us 10 percent off all packages?" The room goes silent. A man at the end of the table, clearly the boss, sporting a sharp tie, an assured look, groomed hair, and square shoulders, leans in and with a strong-sounding, confident voice void of any question says, "Ok here's what we're going to do. We'll use FedEx. They have ground service that will save us 10 percent off all packages." Everyone in the room applauds cheering at his great idea. Remember, it's how you say it as much as what you say.

Consider that how you walk into a room is how you'll be remembered. Do you stand tall with your shoulders back and your chest out? Or are your shoulders slumped as you look around nervously in search of someone that you might know? Ever see a groom in a tuxedo strut right after the wedding ceremony? Now that's confidence.

I attended a networking event recently for a new client and went with an intention of practicing these act-as-if skills. I wore my best outfit and exuded confidence. I walked right up to the CEO, shook his hand confidently, and thanked him for inviting me. I then introduced myself to everyone in the room by walking up to them boldly, shaking their hand and saying, "We haven't met yet. My name is Ann Tardy." It was a networking event, and people were there to meet, so I was determined to meet them all under the auspices of "networking." I began each conversation with "What brought you here?" This is a great way to open a conversation. I shared a few minutes with each person I met, listening intently and intentionally, asking sincere questions to learn more about them, and introducing them to anyone who joined us. I acted confident and curious, two keys to any networking endeavor. When I was ready to move on, I extended my hand in indication that I wanted to close our conversation. I shook hands, smiled confidently, and said genuinely, "It was wonderful to meet you. If you'll excuse me, I'm going to meet some more people at this networking event." I was heartfelt in my opening and my closing. I wasn't lying to leave the conversation; I was merely interested in meeting more people at this "networking" event. Then I walked away and looked for a new person to meet. I approached individuals who were standing alone, and they were visibly happy to have someone to talk to because they were feeling insecure and alone. If there were only people in groups talking, I walked up to the group and worked my way into the conversation. They either included me in their conversation automatically, or they stopped their conversation altogether, at which point I'd say, "Excuse me, I have not had an opportunity to meet you all, and I wanted to do so before the evening ended." If they invited me in to their conversation, then I'd stay. If they didn't, I met each of them and moved on.

The key is that I acted as if I belonged at the event, and I acted as if I were someone they wanted to meet, regardless of how out of place and nervous I felt inside. This acting-as-if attitude gave me the false sense of confidence I needed initially to walk into the room alone, and from there I was able to meet people, and engage in conversation. Suddenly I started feeling extremely self-assured. Soon the whole room knew me, and I knew them, and I no longer had to fake it. I really did feel the confidence I was projecting.

Practice these skills next time you attend any event where you do not know people. Notice that with a goal, like meeting everyone in the room, it is easier to talk to strangers. Now imagine using these skills and talking about something that lights you up, like one of your beat-the-alarm goals.

Your Handshake.

Your handshake is another factor that can contribute to or contaminate early on the level of confidence you have and others have for you. Your handshake should be strong and exude confidence. The web of skin between your finger and your thumb should connect with the other person's web of skin. It feels weak and flimsy when we shake hands with someone who barely grips our hands, and all we get are their fingers. Practice shaking hands with someone close to you, and ask for feedback. Try different handshakes. Notice how your feelings about another person change instantly based on their handshake.

Eye Contact.

"Look into my eyes, pretty girl," said the witch to Snow White. That's what I want to say to some people when they are busy watching my lips instead of my eyes when I am talking (and I know they are not hard of hearing). It's actually distracting and indicates a fear of connecting. Eye contact is so important. Look into another's eyes and notice their eye color. It shows genuine interest in them, and that makes you interesting.

Facial Expressions.

It's so easy to tell how others are feeling based on their facial expressions alone. Your face is the canvas for your feelings. This is good and bad. Bad because if we are not vigilant, the unsure, insecure, doubtful feelings we have will show up on our face. Good because, with practice, we can create facial expressions that exude our confidence and self-assuredness. Notice the facial expressions of other people. See if you can determine based on their face alone how they are feeling. Engage a confidante in a game to see if you can guess what they are feeling based on a facial expression they are making. Then practice in front of the mirror to have that confident, self-assured look. Acting *as if* requires our face to act *as if* as well.

Your Look.

Consider that you are a work of art and just like any art at the Art Institute, your art literally evokes emotions in you and others. My mom always said if you want to feel great, look great. If you are feeling crappy, she'd say, put on your best outfit and make yourself look your best. You will start to feel your best. There are a lot of tools at our disposal to help us look great in order to feel great, so take advantage of them. To this day, my mom projects nothing but confidence using her look, regardless of how she feels on the inside. Her rule of thumb is to always dress one step better than she thinks she should in any situation. She describes her outfits as costumes – she intentionally crafts her look each day so that she projects the image she wants. Her hair is sculpted, her nails are perfectly manicured, and even her car projects a certain "I've made it" look. People actually think she is successful without even knowing her because she projects this image.

As a stay-at-home mom with no college education, my mom strategically created a look that allowed her to act *as if* – act as if she could contribute to the family's income when convincing my dad to support her decision to start a career after 15 years at home; act as if she could be a successful realtor during her interview with a real estate firm; act as if she could sell or buy homes when meeting with potential clients; act as if she could run the whole office successfully when assuming the role of office manager; and act as if she were the realtor of the year when the association of realtors sought applicants for the award and eventually awarded it to her. Her look speaks volumes before she even opens her mouth.

My mom used all of these tools to act *as if* and that allowed her to create the confidence she needed to create the life she wanted. And, as a result, her confidence has given others the confidence in her that they needed to open the doors of opportunity to her in spite of her lack of education and experience. She walked through those doors as if they were damn lucky to have her, and then she proved how fabulous she is. My mom acts *as if* so people think *as if*.

Assuming a certain look may sometimes feel like conforming to society's dictated fashions. In high schools everywhere, there is usually a group of kids that are dubbed "burn-outs" or outcasts. They are easily identified because they assume an all-black look from hair to clothes to shoes to make-up. If asked, they will tell you that they don't want to be judged for what they are wearing like the "cool kids" are judged so they've chosen to wear black. What they fail to realize is that by choosing not to have a look, they are choosing a look, and inevitably, people are judging them. They look as if they don't care so people think they don't care. It's the same in society. You don't have to conform. You just need to acknowledge that every day you choose a look, and that look is your billboard – it is giving a message about you before you even open your mouth. What do you want your billboard to say?

The Pink Ladies and the T-birds in the movie *Grease* chose a look. Olivia Newton John's character in that movie had a look as well, but it wasn't one that projected the coolness required to become a Pink Lady or land a date with a T-bird. In order for her to win the heart of one of the T-birds played by John Travolta, she had to act as if she were that cool, and that required her to change her look. She curled her hair; pierced her ears; applied make-up; wore a slinky, off-the-shoulder, skin-tight, black top; tight leather pants; red high heels; and pretended to smoke a cigarette. She strutted up to John Travolta, whose eyes popped and jaw dropped in shock, gave him the coolest of all looks, and said, "Tell me about it, stud." To which he dropped at her feet feigning a faint, and teen-aged girls around the country screamed in hopeful joy that they too could transform their coolness quotient and win the hearts of the cool guy in school with a little make-up, earrings, and a curling iron.

We are even judged by what we carry when we walk into a meeting. Some women walk in carrying huge, overloaded purses, coffee mugs, boxes of supplies, and computer bags. They are usually judged as the do-er. People will look to them to do whatever gets decided at the meeting. When people walk into a room carrying nothing, they usually come with an air of being a decision maker, not a do-er. Thinkers get paid more than the do-ers. Don't weigh down your look with unnecessary baggage. Start being seen as the thinker, not the do-er.

Your look is one of those wonderful tools you have in your arsenal and at your disposal. Some image consultants even argue that the well-dressed interviewee earns 20 percent more than the person who just throws on a suit for an interview. With a few tweaks, you can easily start looking the part and not wait for your true feelings to catch up. From your clothes to your hair to your teeth to your fingernails, you have absolute control over what others think of you before you even open your mouth. If you ever watched the reality show *Extreme Makeover* or any makeover show, notice how your confidence in a person instantly skyrockets after their look is transformed. They haven't said a word, but because they have a new hairdo or a trimmed beard, fresh make-up, and fitted clothes, their look is instantly altered, which alters their own confidence and our confidence in them. They stand taller with pride as if they've grown a foot.

You have the power to alter others' impression of you in an instant by transforming your own look. Hire an image consultant, get a new hairstyle, get braces, buy new make-up, and learn to create outfits that work for you not against you. My mom's automatic comment about anyone with a bizarre outfit, mismatched clothes, or a slovenly appearance is, "They must not have a mirror." If you choose to look sloppy you will be judged as sloppy. This eats at your self-confidence, taints your ability to act *as if*, closes doors, and inevitably inhibits your chances at creating moxie.

YOUR ACTIONS.

It has been estimated that it takes six encounters to fix a bad first impression. If you yell at a receptionist or flip the bird to the person in the car next to you on the road, people will assume that you are aggressive and hostile. If you fail to ask questions, people will assume that you are a pushover. If you take charge in a meeting, people will believe that you are the leader. When you walk into a room with unquestioning confidence, people will stop and ask, "Who *is* that person?" They have no idea if you are shaking inside, and it never matters if you are.

Start acting the part that you want and stop waiting for someone to grant you the permission to do so. Look at your actions. What are they saying about you? When I am late for a meeting (as I am known to be), I come running in frantic and apologizing for making the other person wait. My actions send the message that I don't manage my time well and that I am rude for not respecting the other person's time. These unspoken messages instantly detract from the relationship, sometimes before it even starts. What actions are you taking that are contributing to or contaminating your communications? If you want to act *as if*, you need to act the part. Act as if you have already been granted permission, given the job or opportunity, or proven your success. When you act as if you are the person to do the job, you are given the opportunity to be the person that does the job.

As a new associate at one of the big accounting firms in Silicon Valley, I found myself engulfed in a sea of cubicles, an employee among many. Since the partners at the firm were not in cubicle-land, I knew they did not have their thumb on the pulse of the low employee morale that permeated the office. I felt compelled to let them know. I began writing memos to the managing partner of the firm. I gave him a window into the world of associates, shared with him what was not working, and provided him a slew of ideas that could spark enthusiasm amongst the employees and motivate them to become a team. I acted as if I had the right to tell him how to deal with his employees. Proving why he was in charge, he responded immediately, clearly hungry for the new perspective and fresh ideas I offered. He scheduled an appointment for us to meet in person.

Over the next few months, I became his source for insight to life among the employees in the firm and his source for ideas to rejuvenate the flat-lined spirit that lingered. I felt a little brazen, as if I was telling the managing partner how to run the firm, and I look back now to that time and think, "Who did I think I was?" (When you've embraced the acting-as-if strategy, this feeling is a great indication that you're in it! The next thing you should ask is, "Who am I not to be here?") I was acting as if this seasoned professional had asked my opinion, and acting as if I had the answers he needed to address his employee morale issues. For me it was bold, brazen, and audacious. For the managing partner it was refreshing. As a result of acting as if I had the right to give my opinion, he gave me the right to give him my opinion on employee issues. To this day, years, firms, and careers later, we remain steadfast friends.

Entrepreneur Barbara Carey made millions with her own bold, brazen, and audacious attitude. With an entrepreneurial spirit running through her veins, she has started many businesses — some successful and some not so successful. She is famous for inventing the hair-ogami product and selling millions. Her philosophy is to never actually build anything before she has a buyer. With a boldness unmatched by most, she approaches retailers like K-Mart and Wal-Mart to sell them on a fabulous new product like a Halloween mask for kids. She walks out of the meeting with an order in her hand for a million masks. Only then on her way out to her car does she call a manufacturer and ask him to start building the product. With an act-as-if attitude, Barbara Carey radiates moxie.

The founder of IBM, Thomas Watson, mastered the art of acting *as if* when he launched one of the most successful companies of all time. Asked to what he attributed the phenomenal success of IBM, he referred to three things. First, before he started the company, he determined what he wanted it to look like when he was done – he created the image. Then he thought about what that company would have to act like to be the company he wanted to create. And finally he ensured the company started acting that way right from the beginning. In other words, Tom Watson started IBM by acting as if he had already made it.

How to Use This Strategy to Create Moxie.

Whatever your beat-the-alarm goal, use acting as if to accelerate the process. When you act *as if*, you fake it 'til you make it. This creates the outward appearance of confidence that you'll need to instill confidence in others. With that confidence, people will grant you the opportunities you need to pursue your beat-the-alarm goals. From there your own confidence will catch up and you will no longer need to fake it. If you want to create moxie, start acting *as if*. Consider how your look, your voice, your body language, your words, your facial expressions, and even your handshake either contribute to or contaminate your own self-confidence, and other's confidence in your attitude. Your ability to act *as if* will determine how far you can open the door and how long it will stay open for you.

Exercises to Act As If

- Practice walking into a room of strangers acting as if you belong. Approach people with your act *as if* and be curious about them with your questions. You will make instantaneous friends and fans.

- Practice expressing your opinions or sharing ideas with confidence and conviction.

- Assess your look — what could you do to create more confidence in yourself and more confidence others have in you?

- Record your voice and listen to it to judge your pitch, inflection, tone, and uptalk. Could you sound more powerful and confident?

- Sing in the shower.

- Declare an expertise in an area and practice telling people that you are an expert.

6

Respond, Don't Just React

*Making Lemonade when
Life Throws You Lemons*

Things happen to us every day, and they rarely go as we plan, but when we are committed, it doesn't matter what happens. We'll find a way to achieve our beat-the-alarm goal anyway. That's when we move from reaction to response. Reacting is the cloud that hangs over us; responding is the silver lining. Reacting is dropping the lemons that life tosses us; responding is catching the lemons and making lemonade. Reacting is crying; responding is doing something about it. The secret is to first cry and then ask why. Gain wisdom from tragedy, not a hall pass. Once we learn from our mistakes, we can do something about them and keep moving forward.

LEARNING TO ROLL.

While we need to express our disappointment, frustration, anger, and upset, we also need to learn to put life into perspective and stop reacting so quickly. Too often we lose our temper because of something that we later realize was insignificant in the bigger picture. For instance, a scratch on the door of his new BMW sent Joey through the roof. His anger was loud and seemed never-ending. He spent over four hours screaming and yelling at everyone in his path over the scratch on his new car door. His bad mood impacted his family's mood and stilted all conversation thereby ruining their dinner. The next morning on the way to the office, another car smashed into the side of that slightly scratched door of his brand new car. Suddenly, Joey longed for the tiny scratch.

Jillie is 6 and while once a master at the pout, her dad has taught her to master the art of rolling. When she realized that a situation was not going her way, her immediate reaction was to drop her head, slump her shoulders, sadden her eyes, pop out her bottom lip, and go quiet. For example, when her brother ate the last chocolate chip cookie, she struggled to express her upset so she pouted. And everyone would naturally pour attention on this sweet, adorable little girl to try unsuccessfully to fix the situation and make her happy again. Eventually, the only recourse was to ignore her for a while and let her work her way out of it. It became a game.

While her dad was grateful that she did not express her frustration with a temper tantrum, he wanted to give her life-coping skills. He created a way to teach Jillie to express her upset or frustration using words, to put the situation into perspective, and to find a way to move past the disappointment more quickly. They began a new game. Every time something upset Jillie, she would raise her right hand and declare, "I'm going to pout now," and then he timed her to see how fast she could come up with a solution on her own and roll out of her pout. Sometimes she came up with great alternatives to the last chocolate chip cookie. Sometimes she even decided that it no longer mattered to her. Other times, she completely forgot about what originally upset her altogether. The gift he gave his daughter was the art of the roll couched in the form of a game. What we all would have given to have had that lesson at the age of 6.

We tend to get easily thrown off when we have an expectation of how something is supposed to happen but doesn't because an unpredictable circumstance gets in the way. For instance, on the way to the airport for your honeymoon, the sky opens up, and it begins to pour. If you have set your expectations such that the honeymoon will only be perfect if every detail is perfect, then the rain will throw you for a loop causing you to react unnecessarily. Road rage is often born over the small stuff. Or we get upset when someone says "No" to our request. We all hate hearing the word "No."It triggers something in us as if they are rejecting us personally with their "No."

Instead of getting thrown for a loop, try a few different approaches to roll past the small stuff quickly and get back to the significant stuff. When someone says "No," ask them "Why?" This will buy you a response from which you can respond, as well as time to think. Next, respond with, "I'm confused. Help me understand. I thought..." and then state what you thought the situation was supposed to be. This approach was made famous in my family by my dad who used it often in his very successful sales career. For example, suppose you ask someone for a lower price and they say "No, my product is worth it." You can respond first by asking "Why?" They should be able to explain why they think their product is worth its price. You can then say, "I'm confused. Help me understand. I thought there was a sale going on today." Again, it keeps you calm, keeps the conversation alive, and keeps you in the game. You can use the "I'm confused. Help me understand" line to keep you calm in many situations where someone gives you an answer you don't agree with or expect.

When something happens to you, on the other hand, try this approach to roll with it. Imagine yourself floating above the Earth looking at the billions of people enduring all sorts of existences. Then ask yourself if the scratch on the car door or the downpour really matters. Alternatively, imagine that you are 10 years into the future and ask yourself if in 10 years you will care any more about the scratch on the car door or the rainy day. If it doesn't matter, then it's an insignificant punch. Let's save our energy and roll right past it.

Cry.

If it's not something to easily roll past, then it's something to cry about, so cry. Growing up, my mom would always encourage us to cry when we were upset. She said crying lets us know that we are feeling sad, and only because we know when we are sad will we be able to know when we are happy. Crying is our expression of upset. We feel frustrated. It wells up inside us. We think, "Why me? Why did this happen to me?" It's perfectlyokay to be upset, disappointed, frustrated, and mad at ourselves or the world, as long as we don't stay there very long. People with moxie experience disappointment, failures, and upsets all the time. The difference is that while the rest of the world is stuck in their tears, people with moxie dry their eyes quickly so they can see where they're going next.

Your version of the cry may include all-out sobbing and streams of tears. Or it may look like pouting, sulking, shouting, or screaming. Whatever the form it takes, the important part is that you are expressing it and getting it out of your system completely, in a non-destructive manner. Some ways that you could express your cry include going for a walk or a run, counting to 100, journaling, writing an angry letter that you don't send, calling your therapist or a best friend (or my mom!), going to the movies, reading a book, getting a massage, or just going to bed and starting over tomorrow.

How you choose to cry and for how long will depend on the situation, and how important it was to you. Too often people express their upset by turning to alcohol, cigarettes, food, drugs, or shopping. The problem with these expressions is that they don't express upset, they numb it. Numbing it doesn't move us forward; it stagnates us. Your reaction to a speeding ticket will likely be different and much shorter than your reaction to the death of a family member or the loss of your job. In exercise, the unofficial way to test your fitness level is by how fast you can recover your heart rate after a strenuous workout. In life, the test is how fast you can recover your spirit. To move through upset quickly, find a constructive way to "cry" and give yourself permission to feel bad in the moment.

Ask Why.

Once we have had a good cry, we need to move on towards our beat-the-alarm goal, but that requires us to first look at what happened and ask why. This entails looking at our role in that answer. Only when we understand what happened will we have the tools to move forward more intelligently. It's impossible to learn if we don't examine the past. When we don't ask why, we make up reasons in our head, and our make-believe could lead us down the wrong path altogether.

When you ask "Why?" be prepared for the answer. Our first instinct is to defend our actions or inactions, justify, or make excuses. But all of that is just reacting; it's not responding. You may not like the answer you get when you ask "Why?" You may want to argue, defend, stomp around, and pout that life isn't fair, and you would be right; life probably wasn't fair to you. But if you want to live a life of moxie, you cannot wallow in all the ways that life is not fair. There is no moxie in "life is not fair." Just accept that the answer is the answer.

If you did not get the promotion and the reason your boss gave you seems unfounded, don't spend time fighting her reasoning. Just seek to understand it. Only from there can you respond directly and ensure a chance at changing the situation going forward. If your house burned down, there is no sense arguing that it should not have burned down. It did. The *why* will be important when you build your next house. If you are playing a baseball game and the umpire calls the ball out, don't scream at the umpire about his poor eyesight. Have you ever seen an umpire change his mind about a call because a player got in his face and screamed at him? Instead, seek to understand not only the rules of the game, but the umpire. If you are stuck screaming or crying you will miss out on discovering the *why*. It's nearly impossible to learn anything without discovering the *why*.

The next part of asking why is looking at our role in the answer. This is equally as tough because no one likes to be at fault. And regardless of the situation, it's never easy to admit that we were wrong. Remember Fonzi on the popular television show *Happy Days*? He was the coolest guy around, and because of that he had the hardest time admitting that he was wrong. In fact, much audience laughter was generated by his unsuccessful attempts to say the words, "I was wrong." It usually came out as "I was wr- wr- wr- wrooong." And he would then have to sit down exhausted by what he just said.

We are great at pointing fingers, blaming others, and producing victims out of ourselves or culprits out of others. Again, it's just another form of crying. So, it's understandable as an immediate reaction, but then we need to stop. And the longer we do it, the more we need to clean up when we're ready to move on. Pointing fingers does not allow us to respond, and there's definitely no moxie in it. When we blame someone else or something else for what happened to us, it's as if we are standing in cement glued to a position and unable to move forward. Instead we need to ask, what is our contribution to the current situation? What did we do or not do that contributed to the mistake, failure, circumstances, black cloud, or lemons. If we did not do, or fail to do, anything to cause the disappointment, then what are we not doing right now that is causing us to be stuck here? It could be that our failure to respond is keeping us stuck.

We can learn a lot from the innovation failures of corporations and their responses. Successful companies ask "why" in order to gather important information that allows them to make better products or provide better services. Unsuccessful companies ask "why" only for the purpose of defending their failed product or service or blaming someone or something else for the failure. No matter how much they defend or point fingers, it doesn't increase sales.

In 1985 after a lot of research and taste-testing, Coca-Cola rolled out "New Coke," a new formula promising to reenergize its lethargic brand. They could not possibly have predicted the firestorm of consumer protests that ensued. New Coke was pulled 79 days later. Stunned, the company scratched its collective head in disbelief. It wasn't foreseeable; it was a disaster; and it certainly wasn't fair. However, in order to move forward and salvage the consumer loyalty, they needed to respond, and respond quickly. They cried a corporate cry, and then they immediately asked why. They learned that consumers may have liked the new formula, but they had a love affair with the original taste. With that valuable information, Coca-Cola re-launched the original Coke with a huge PR initiative and to great consumer applause.

McDonald's had a similar learning experience in 1962. Founder Ray Kroc wanted to create a meatless sandwich for Catholic Chicagoans who avoided eating meat on Fridays. And create he did. He proudly released the Hula Burger, a cheese-topped grilled pineapple on a bun. But consumers did not bite—literally. Disappointed, Ray Kroc asked why. He learned that consumers' commitment to meatless Fridays did not translate into a willingness to give up substance in favor of an off-the-wall option. A year later McDonald's invented a tastier, less wacky alternative for hamburger-free Fridays: the Filet-O-Fish, now a staple on the McDonald's menu.

In 1982 Tylenol taught all corporations the art of responding after asking "why" when their product became the victim of product tampering. Seven people in the Chicagoland suburbs died as a result of taking Tylenol laced with cyanide. Without wasting a moment to point a finger, Tylenol responded. They immediately pulled all product from retailers' shelves, employed tamper-evident packaging on all products, and invented the first inherently tamper-proof capsule.

FAIL FORWARD.

It'sokay to take a risk and fail; it's not okay to fail and not learn. From losing your job to getting divorced, you may vacillate between a woeful "why me" and "life isn't fair" to an emotional outrage at yourself or another – all understandable reactions. Once you get past the crying and you understand the *why* it happened, it's time to look at what you learned. You may have made a mistake in choosing the wrong employer or the wrong spouse. What will you do differently next time to choose better? Also, it's important to look at the good things that did come out of the experience. Perhaps you learned what you want in a future employer or a future spouse that fit well with your goals and personality. Perhaps you learned more about the kind of person you are in these situations. If nothing else, you know what you don't want next time you take a job or get married. Failures are only failures if we don't learn from them.

Breakthroughs in research depend on failures because companies learn from these failures and only then can they get closer to the solution. As a child, the only way we learn to walk is to try, fall down, learn, and try again. Thomas Edison was known for celebrating the several thousand things that he knew wouldn't work as a result of all of his experiments. And Winston Churchill acknowledged that in order to succeed we must keep our enthusiasm in spite of the inevitable failures.

Henry Ford appreciated failure because it gave him the opportunity to begin again more intelligently. Out of one of Ford Motor Company's failures was born a timeless treasure. In 1957, Ford rolled out the Edsel amid self-generated excitement and anticipation. But it flopped. Customers disliked the car immediately. Some said it was too big; some said it was too expensive; others said the styling was too unique. The public even ridiculed the stodgy name. Realizing its failure, Ford stopped production after less than 3,000 cars. Through extensive customer research, they sought to learn from their mistake. They discovered that customers wanted style and affordability. In 1964, Ford's flop gave birth to the legendary Ford Mustang.

Celebrate Smart Mistakes.

Thomas Edison attempted more than 2,000 experiments before he successfully created the first light bulb. R.H. Macy tried seven different times to open his store *Macy's* in New York before it finally caught on. Bill Hewlett and Dave Packard, the founders of computer giant Hewlett-Packard, first invented a lettuce-picking machine and an electric weight-loss machine, both of which failed miserably. Bill Gates and Paul Allen, co-founders of software giant Microsoft, first launched Traf-O-Data, an unsuccessful business that analyzed automobile traffic flow. In 1920 Walt Disney and animator Ub Iwerks opened a cartoon production company named Iwerks-Disney Commercial Artists which collapsed after just one month. All of these famous entrepreneurs became wildly successful, but only because they failed forward. They learned from their mistakes and failures and tried again with a different approach.

Reflecting on extraordinary careers in sports, we see that players also celebrate their smart mistakes. They miss many shots, goals, and touchdowns, lose many games, and are often entrusted to take the game-winning shot, goal or touchdown only to miss. Arguably even the all-time greats fail over and over and over again in their careers, but they succeed precisely because of how much they fail – those failures teach them what they need to do to win.

What failures and mistakes are you focusing on in your life? What if you changed the focus from the failure to the lesson? What lessons have you learned? Celebrate the mistakes and be grateful for the lessons. Keep making mistakes – that's the only way we learn; just commit to making new mistakes.

Great innovative companies employ a formula for embracing failures that works just as well for our personal lives. To prevent failures and their valuable lessons from being swept under the rug, innovative companies carve out time for reflection. Let's do the same. Create a lesson journal and start documenting all the great lessons you've learned in your life, on your job, with your significant other, and in raising your kids. Innovative companies also practice flexibility in meeting goals. They tend to ignore the hard and fast deadlines set at the outset as merely educated guesses. Similarly, set yourself up for success by moving towards the beat-the-alarm goal but being willing to move the goalposts if necessary as you discover new information. When we set stretch beat-the-alarm goals, like losing 50 pounds, starting a business or changing careers, our risk of failure is higher. As you head down the path, don't give up just because you discover you're not going to make the exact deadline. Be flexible. You can still win. You will learn information along the way that will help you achieve the goal but may cause a shift in the deadline. (Just be cautious not to set a beat-the-alarm goal with the intention of moving the goal posts.)

Innovative companies also encourage employees to share their failures. They start with the front-line leaders who are the first to say, "I made a mistake." Imagine what we could learn from our friends and family if we similarly shared our mistakes and our lessons, instead of the typical gripe about what happened to us and who was to blame. What if you took on failure like a game and challenged yourself to fail often and a lot, as long as you never failed at the same thing twice? What fun that would be! "So, John, how are you doing?" "I'm doing great; I failed again today!" That sounds funny, doesn't it? But what if we changed the words? Would it be easier to say, "I'm doing great, I learned something new today!"? An entrepreneurial professor at Harvard Business School once said that it takes most successful entrepreneurs five years to figure out their business model, during which time they make a lot of mistakes. Their success lies in not making the same mistake twice.

Finally, managers of innovative companies design performance-management systems that reward risk-taking. They encourage their employees to try new things and to try again and again. They celebrate failures that teach something new. We celebrate when kids try crawling and walking even when they fall down. It's time we celebrate our own smart failures in a similar way by rewarding ourselves for taking risks. When we try and we fail, we still have the opportunity to learn; but when we fail to even try, we miss out on all that may be available to us.

LEARN TO BOUNCE.

Learning to bounce is essential to having moxie. It'sokayto react to whatever happened – cry away! – but the key to creating moxie is to take those lessons we learned from asking why, celebrate our smart mistakes, and move forward. No matter what, always ask, "What did I learn and what can I do from here?" When we move the focus from what happened to what can I do about it, we are able to move more quickly through life's disappointments. The art of the bounce has two parts – getting back up and then doing something. The first part is not getting stopped by whatever happened to us. The second part is taking the next step by acting on what we've learned; it's responding to the "why" after the cry.

The Weebles were masterful at the art of the bounce. The Weeble is a child's toy from the late 1970s in the shape of an egg that wobbled back and forth and never fell down. The egg-shaped character had a human face, clothes and hands painted on it, and a round, heavier lower half in place of its legs. When you knocked it over, it rolled right back to an upright position. Their theme was "Weebles wobble, but they don't fall down." Let's study the Weebles so that when life knocks you down, you have no choice but to get back up.

Abraham Lincoln also mastered the art of the bounce, and as a result, rests in history as a man of perseverance. Lincoln helped support his family by leaving school and working full time at a young age. As a result, he received less than one year of formal education in his life. Instead of letting this circumstance stop him, he educated himself and eventually became a lawyer. He was very passionate about the potential of the government, and in order to make a significant impact in this arena, he entered politics. Determined to achieve a high position in government, the presidency became his burning desire. Unfortunately, he was challenged by several business and political setbacks. Within one decade, he was defeated in his first run for Illinois legislature, his legal practice went bankrupt, he had a nervous breakdown, and although he was elected to the Illinois Congress, he lost his election to the U.S. Congress. After trying again, he finally won the election to the U.S. Congress and served a term. He then took five years off from politics to reassess his failures. Reinvigorated, he ran for the U.S. Senate and lost; two years later he ran for the vice presidency of the United States and lost; another two years passed before he ran for the U.S. Senate again and lost; and finally after another two years, he ran for the presidency of the United States and won. Most people would have given up long before. Not Lincoln. He knew how to bounce.

While the first part of bouncing requires us to get back up, the second part entails shifting the focus from what happened and what you learned to what action you can take after you get back up. When we bounce, we take action based on the information we learned from asking why. For instance, suppose you are a salesperson pitching your product to a potential customer and she just said "No." If you walk away annoyed at her, the product, or your sales skills, you forgot to bounce. On the other hand, if you ask her why and she explains that she doesn't like the color, then you have the opportunity to respond and show her that there are five other colors from which to choose. Only when you discover the reason behind her "No" are you able to specifically address her "No" and take action from there. That's responding.

Our résumés, like our obituaries, demand that we bounce. When we create a résumé, we summarize our work experience with each employer in only a few sentences. We document our accomplishments, our what-we-did-about-its. There is no room to document what happened, how unfair it was, how frustrated we felt, the curve balls, the potholes, or the upsets we experienced. We can only show how we moved forward again and again. Obituaries similarly give us perspective on our lives. When your family writes up the three paragraphs for the local paper to print on your life, they won't write about the time you lost a job or didn't get promoted, or the time you got a DUI or tried to start a business but failed. They only write what you did in your life after those defeats.

Your Own Bounce.

The way you bounce is up to you. You may bounce by trying again with a different approach, or you may bounce by trying something new altogether. Either way, bouncing requires that we get back up, learn something, and then take action. The famous movie producer Steven Spielberg bounced by trying the academic way and then his own way. He recalls high school as one of the worst experiences of his life. School may not have been for him, but life certainly was. After a childhood of making films and an award-winning movie by the time he was 13, he applied to UCLA's film school and the USC School of Cinema-Television three separate times and was rejected each time on the basis of his low high school grades. Spielberg found another avenue to get the education and experience he needed. He entered California State University and quickly landed himself an unpaid three-day-a week internship at Universal Studios. Spielberg went on to produce extraordinary and timeless movies such as *Jaws*, *E.T.*, and *Jurassic Park*.

Even Michael Jordan, one of the greatest basketball players of all time, had to learn to bounce – and not just a basketball – after his dream of playing professional basketball was threatened early on. As a sophomore on the varsity high school basketball team, he was cut during his sophomore year on the basis that he was underdeveloped. Jordan spent the following summer training rigorously to rejoin the team. He went on to lead his senior year of basketball in high school and was selected to McDonald's All-American Team. The real failure in life is when people are close to success but give up before they realize it. Steven Spielberg and Michael Jordan realized success because they tried again and again after meeting disappointments on their journey.

As Michael Jordan showed us, taking action requires responding to the *why*. This is a particularly great approach to have with you when discussing a raise with your boss. If your boss says "No" and you walk away upset at him, the company, or your abilities, then you have lost out on the opportunity to learn and you have hindered your ability to respond. Whenever you hear the word "No," ask "Why?" Elicit from your boss more information that you can use to move forward. Your boss may say that he is concerned about the company's budget or about your performance. Knowing what concerns him is valuable information. From here you can respond accordingly. Notice how different this approach is to one in which you react to your boss' "No" by storming out of his office cursing him, the company, or yourself. By asking "Why?" you obtain the ammunition you need to respond, and your response will include addressing his concerns.

I learned the art of the bounce while creating one of my greatest moxie moments. After moving to California and spending time at one of the big accounting firms, I was ready to practice law. I began interviewing at the largest and oldest law firm in California, Pillsbury Madison & Sutro. From the moment I stepped into their offices, I wanted to work for them. I interviewed for four months and fell in love with everyone I met – from the Human Resources assistant, to the receptionist, to the partners, to the associates. They kept calling me back to meet more attorneys. By the end of the four months I had met every attorney in their Silicon Valley office. The more I met, the more I wanted to belong to this tribe.

On Christmas Eve, I received a phone call from the Human Resources department. They decided not to offer me a job. Stunned, I swallowed back tears and asked her why. She said that the firm felt that I did not have enough experience. I couldn't believe it. I hung up the phone, cried, and proceeded to sulk the remainder of the holiday weekend about how unfair it was. As the New Year rolled around, I was done sulking and started asking myself what I was going to do next. I knew I wanted to join a law firm; if it wasn't Pillsbury, then I was going to find another firm to launch my legal career.

But I felt that I was not done dancing with Pillsbury. I felt a need to respond to their concern that I did not have enough experience. I addressed their concern in a letter I wrote to one of the partners. I thanked her for the opportunity to interview and let her know that I understood the firm's concern. Then I explained the 15 ways I was going to get the experience they felt

I lacked and that then I'd be back to work for Pillsbury. My list included such things as: work for another firm to get the requisite experience, take some more classes, and work for Pillsbury for free for three months. After mailing the letter, I continued my journey to launch my new career. I sent out resumes, wrote letters, and networked.

A few weeks after sending my letter to Pillsbury, I received a phone call from the managing partner's secretary. He wanted to meet me for breakfast. Skeptical and prepared for a consolation prize, I agreed. As we sat down he said, "Your letter made its way to my desk, and after reading it, I realize that we obviously made a mistake. We'd like to offer you a job." Choking back more tears, I accepted. Had I taken their initial "No" and walked away defeated, I would have missed out on the opportunity that just needed to be uncovered. Instead, I asked why, responded to their concern, and bounced my way into the best job I've ever had.

BLAME.

Our litigious society encourages the blaming of others. It's because of our natural tendency to point fingers that television shows like Judge Wapner and Judge Judy thrive. It's because of our failure to take responsibility that we hear too often of lawsuits in which an overweight, unhealthy adult sues a fast food restaurant for his obesity. It's easier to blame McDonald's than to choose to eat better, go to the gym every morning, and commit to a healthy lifestyle. Blaming others particularly flourishes in divorce court. When one spouse is adulterous, it is easier to point the finger at the jerk than to consider that both spouses allowed the relationship to deteriorate, and that one spouse chose to be a coward by avoiding the situation with an affair. An affair is rarely the reason a marriage ends – it's usually just a sign that something else is wrong.

People usually fail to bounce because we are too busy blaming other people, including ourselves, for what happened. There's no moxie in blaming anyone, including yourself. It is so much easier to point the finger at another person and blame them for how your life turned out. From alcoholic parents to cheating spouses to mean bosses, it may feel great to blame them in the moment, but it's the reason there is no bounce in your ball. Driving through life by looking through the rear view mirror causes us to take the self-pity route. We miss out on learnings and opportunities that may be right in front of us. We waste time wallowing in the what-happened and the why-me. Don't waste your life this way. If there is no bounce in your ball, consider who you are blaming for your life and start taking responsibility for making it the way you want. Start driving through the front windshield and only use the rear view mirror to reflect on how far you've come.

EXCUSES.

Another way that we take the air out of our bounce is by weighing it down with excuses and feelings. "I would, but…" The "but" is the nail in the rubber ball. If you find yourself getting stuck, look at the excuses you have for why you can't move forward. If you are committed to running the race or losing the weight, there *are* no excuses. If it's raining, go to the gym instead. If it's too cold, bundle up. If you're too tired, take a nap later. If you're too busy, make the time. Stop using excuses – your life is at stake!

J.K. Rowling was not even slowed down by the myriad of excuses that her life presented. When Oxford turned her down, she studied French and Classics at the University of Exeter. Soon after graduating, her love of literature inspired her to create the young character Harry Potter. She was bringing life to Harry Potter when her mom lost her own life after a 10-year battle with multiple sclerosis. Shortly thereafter Rowling left London to teach English in Portugal where she met and married a Portuguese television journalist. Right after their child was born, her husband threw them both out of the house, so Rowling and her daughter moved to Scotland to be near her sister. Throughout this journey, Rowling kept writing about Harry Potter in spite of her own drama. Unemployed and living on welfare, she completed her first novel, *Harry Potter and the Sorcerer's Stone,* during her daughter's naps. In the face of all that life threw her way, she didn't use excuses as her crutch; instead she kept moving forward on her beat-the-alarm goals. She may have cried often, but she didn't wallow in what happened, who was to blame, or how she ended up in her situation. Instead, she did what she needed to do to move forward and is now one of the wealthiest women in the world. That's moxie.

The more you create moxie in your life, the more that excuses will make you cringe. Eventually you will begin tuning them out altogether. When people drone on and on with their excuses, you will only hear them like cartoon child *Charlie Brown* and his friends heard adults: "wha wha wha wha wha wha wha wha." When their lips are done moving you will look at them, and the moxie in you will automatically respond, "So, what are you going to do about it?"

MAKE LEMONADE.

When life throws you lemons, moxie says make lemonade. Sometimes we can't move forward in the *way* we want to, but we can always move forward. When we stay focused on and committed to our overall missions and beat-the-alarm goals, it doesn't matter that life threw us a few lemons; it matters that we know how to make lemonade.

Pfizer's lemonade made them millions of dollars and a household name. In 1991 Pfizer tested on humans, a drug called Sildenafil, to treat chest pain. To their disappointment, they discovered that the drug was ineffective at treating this condition. To their delight, however, they also discovered that patients were experiencing a side effect — erections. Recognizing the enormous potential, Pfizer began testing the drug to treat erectile dysfunction, and in 1998 released Viagra, the first drug of its kind to give people with impotence a second chance at intimate relationships.

Similarly, Emily made lemonade after androgen alopecia left her with noticeable hair loss at a young age. Emily spent years in various forms of recluse, ashamed of her situation. She soon realized that instead of hiding, she had an opportunity to help other people who similarly suffered. Emily launched the appropriately named *Moxie Parlour* in San Francisco, a fabulous hair salon that also offers private appointments to provide extra support for people who suffer from hair loss. Emily used her own moxie to turn a situation ripe with "why me" into one that inspires and empowers her as well as hundreds of others who have spent years enduring shame.

Martha Stewart created an empire out of her lemons. She first used her moxie to develop a business out of her flair for restoring, decorating, homemaking, and entertaining. In the 80s Martha published books on these topics and in 1990 launched the *Martha Stewart Living* magazine. In 1997 she formed Martha Stewart Omnimedia, home of the Martha Stewart brand and all television, print, and merchandising businesses. Her business thrived until 2002 when Martha was accused of insider trading by the Securities and Exchange Commission. The accusations and her subsequent conviction in 2004 impacted her business and her spirits greatly. Upon her release from prison in 2005, however, Martha came back fighting. She launched a highly publicized comeback, including the release of new books, television appearances, a new upscale line of homewares for Macy's, a new line of ready-made home furnishings for K-mart, and a satellite radio call-in show hosted by Martha herself. When handed a bushel of lemons, Martha had a choice, and she chose to use her moxie to not only make lemonade but open a lemonade stand.

Many amazing individuals have become famous because of the lemonade they created. Christopher Reeve showed Superman-strength both on and off the screen when a horse-riding accident left him a paraplegic. He used his situation to fight for stem cell research. Susan G. Komen's family set up a foundation to fight breast cancer, the disease that took Susan's life, and as a result has brought awareness and millions of dollars to research the cause. After John Walsh's son was abducted and murdered, he founded the National Center for Missing and Exploited Children and from this advocacy was recruited to host the television program, *America's Most Wanted* to help other parents protect their children. Elizabeth Glaser, who contracted HIV through a blood transfusion, spent her life raising awareness and money to fight AIDS. James Brady, who was shot and paralyzed as a Secret Service agent protecting President Reagan, used his situation to fight for gun control. Being born in Ghana, West Africa with a deformed right leg didn't stop Emmanuel from writing to the Challenged Athletes Foundation (CAF) to request a bicycle to ride across his country to disprove the cruel stereotypes about disabled people. He received the bike and a prosthetic leg, both of which game him the freedom to walk, ride, and inspire a nation with his resilience and perseverance. Even the Special Olympics were born out of a group of individuals who were thrown lemons and made lemonade. The difference between these people and millions of others that suffer the toss of lemons is that they engaged their moxie to respond, not just react. Instead of blaming the world for their suffering, they worked to make the world a better place.

HOW TO USE THIS STRATEGY TO CREATE MOXIE.

What is stopping you from having everything you want? What excuses are you allowing to get in the way? What has happened and what could you make happen? Turn a reaction into a response by asking "Why?" Stop blaming others, stop making excuses, and stop being defensive. What lemons has life thrown you? How can you make lemonade? Once you have identified your reasons to beat the alarm clock, it won't matter that the path is riddled with potholes and speed bumps. It only matters that you keep moving forward in pursuit of those beat-the-alarm goals.

Exercises to Respond, Don't Just React.

- Describe a mistake you made that you learned from — what did you learn?

- What is one of your biggest failures and what do you celebrate about it?

- Describe something that happened to you from which you made lemonade out of lemons.

- What has happened to you recently that has completely thrown you off your path?

- What is something that you could do next?

STRATEGY NO.

Ask

. . . .

Getting What You Need and Want

Your success and happiness in life depend on your ability to ask—early, often, and for everything. When we ask for things we need and want, we gain self-worth and confidence. And surprisingly, we usually get what we ask for, or at least the information we need to move forward. Even with a "No" looming overhead, people with moxie are cognizant that to get where they want to go, they need to ask. They know their value, ask powerfully, and respond accordingly. As a result, they move closer to their beat-the-alarm goals, while the rest of the world walks around in circles avoiding the "ask" for fear of rejection. Moxie never eradicates the fear that looms behind the ask, but moxie is so much louder that you'll soon forget the fear even has a voice.

WHAT IF.

The "what if" swirling around in our heads is like a hurricane that destroys everything in its path. We need something from someone, and yet instead of asking, we're busy playing out the "what ifs" in our head — what if they say "No"? What if I appear greedy? What if they laugh? What if they don't like me? What if I look incompetent? What if I don't get what I need? Instead of asking we get stuck analyzing all of the "what ifs." When we are

153

so focused on our beat-the-alarm goal, however, we don't give the what-ifs any power. We treat them as merely informational tools.

In his autobiography *Pursuit of Happyness,* Chris Gardner (played by Will Smith in the movie by the same name) teaches us the power of desire over the fear of rejection. At a critical turning point in his life, Chris was a desperate salesman struggling to make ends meet, spending six months homeless while raising his son by himself, wondering how to put food on the table, and aiming for the happiness that he was sure was just around the corner. One day in a parking lot, a shiny red convertible Ferrari was in search of a spot and Chris seized the moment. Wrought with a desire to be driving that car and living the life that goes with it, Chris wanted to know how the driver got there. So, he asked. He called out to the driver and offered him his parking spot in exchange for answers to two questions. He asked the man what he did for a living and how he did it. The happy, dapper man laughed jovially and agreed. He shared with Chris that for a living he was a stockbroker, and then, over lunch, he offered to explain how he did it. With those two questions, Chris' world of possibilities opened up, and he changed the course of his life forever. Chris eventually became a stockbroker with Dean Witter in spite of his lack of education, experience, or connections. What he didn't lack was moxie.

If the "what ifs" were swirling in Chris' head, he paid them no attention. He was intensely driven by a need to make more money to support his son. He didn't have to ask those two questions at all. He could have just looked longingly at the Ferrari and thought how lucky the man must be. Instead he looked at the driver and thought, how do I get to where this guy is? He could have walked away with those questions still churning in his head. But instead he asked the questions of the only person that could answer – the driver of the Ferrari. Of course, the guy could have been a jerk; or he could have scoffed at Chris or poked fun at him. He also could have been the auto mechanic for the car or a car salesman, neither with any information whatsoever to answer Chris' questions. But Chris would never know unless he pushed the "what ifs" aside and asked anyway.

As you clutch your beat-the-alarm goals, what are the "what ifs" that are holding you back from asking for what you want or need to move forward? When your beat-the-alarm goals are so exciting and inspiring to you, your commitment to achieve them will become more important than any concern or fear you have about asking. Perhaps you fear rejection like the rest of us or you just hate the idea of asking for help because it makes you feel weak. You may even be concerned that your relationship with another person will be tainted if you ask for more. For example, suppose you just completed a successful job interview and the employer has placed a generous offer on the table. Do you ask for more or are you concerned that asking for more will change the employer's mind causing them to retract their offer? That depends on how committed you are to your beat-the-alarm goal. If your beat-the-alarm goal is to put your children through college, and the salary that was offered, regardless of how generous, is not going to enable you to do so, then you ask.

If you do not have any beat-the-alarm goals, or you have them but they are not energizing you, then you might not ask at all for fear the employer will retract the offer. Before you walk away from an opportunity to ask (and possibly earn more), however, consider that you can approach this powerfully. You could preface your ask with a statement that underlines your self-respect and confirms their decision to hire you. You could say, "I am honored for the opportunity to work with you at this company. Before I accept, I need to let you know that I am working on some huge goals in my life, one of which involves this position. So to achieve all that I am set out to do, I need to ask for more money. This is what I am thinking..." Then if they say "No," you could find out what it will take to earn that kind of money from them in the future.

The feelings of fear that are triggered by the "what ifs" will never go away completely, but their paralyzing impact decreases when not asking becomes worse than being rejected or not getting the assistance you need. When we don't ask we miss out on the opportunity to move forward with a "Yes" or the rich market research that accompanies a "No." Either one will get you closer to your beat-the-alarm goals.

You Never Know Until You Ask.

If we don't ask, we don't get. As my mom would say, "What's the worst that can happen?" They can say "No." We already know what we have; we have no idea what we could get. But we need to ask to find out. We'll never know until we ask.

Didi Conn landed the part of Frenchy in the 1978 movie *Grease* because she asked. When the auditions were announced, interested actors were allowed to pick up their lines for the audition at Paramount Pictures' gatehouse. When she arrived, the guard handed her two pages with her lines for the audition. Without the whole script, she was clueless as to what the movie was about and she was at a loss for how her character was supposed to fit in. Didi really wanted to be an actress and saw this as an opportunity if she could land this role. She also knew that to do so she would have to stand out and show the producers how she would add value to the movie; and that required an understanding of how her role fit into the whole movie. Noticing the movie's full script on the desk in the gatehouse behind the guard, she asked him if she could sit right there in the gatehouse and read it. He agreed. With a clear picture of the part for which she was auditioning, Didi arrived at the audition with her hair in a '60s-style colorful red bouffant as was called for by the character Frenchy. The producers laughed and knew instantly that Didi was the perfect person for the part. Didi was clear about her beat-the-alarm goal to be an actress and then asked the guard for what she needed to achieve that goal. That's moxie.

Hattie knew the power of you-never-know-until-you-ask. She was 20 during World War II and a pilot in the military. She wanted to join an all-male flying club in California, so she saved up her money for the new member fees. Cognizant that she'd be breaking a mold, Hattie approached the group and asked to become a member of this all-male faction. The flying club took a vote, and the members voted 50-1 in favor of letting her into the group, especially in light of the fact that she had the money for the fees at a time when money was scarce. Hattie could have assumed that because they didn't have any women members they must not allow women into the group. On this assumption she could have chosen not to approach them at all. Instead she decided to ask. She never would have known if she hadn't asked. As a bonus to this true story, a year after she joined the club, Hattie married the only man who voted against admitting her.

Seeking a meaningful part-time job during high school, I learned my first lesson in you-never-know-until-you-ask. It was the middle of the semester of my all-time favorite elective class, Business Law. I had fallen in love with the class and was ready to become a lawyer at the ripe old age of 16. I needed a part-time job for the summer, and although practicing law as a high school junior was not an option, I didn't want to wait for a law degree to get more exposure. So, I wrote a letter to every law firm in the tri-city area in which we lived, asking for a part-time job. I received many kind rejections and one interview. That one interview resulted in a wonderful two-year experience in a small-town law practice. It would have been easy to be stopped with the thought that no one would ever hire me. But I was so excited about my ambition to become a lawyer that I didn't even stop to give that fear any credence. I just thought I'd ask.

KNOW YOUR VALUE.

In order to ask powerfully, we need to know our value. Otherwise, we risk surrendering all power to the other side. Knowing our value requires that we research it using third-party evidence and empirical data and then communicate it to others. For example, if you are looking at your value as an employee and wish to start a conversation about your salary, third-party data could include salary surveys found on the Internet, others' experience in similar positions in your industry or your geographic location, and a recruiter's knowledge of the market. You can also determine your value by looking at your education, experience, contributions to other companies, and, if you are seeking a raise, your contributions to your current employer. Likewise, if you are looking at the value of your products or services, third-party data will include the price of competing products and services, your differentiating factors, the problems you solve, and success stories and testimonials.

Once you have a sense of your value using third-party data and empirical evidence, you need to communicate it. Communicating includes documenting the evidence for yourself and sharing it with the party you are about to ask. When you are interviewing, you communicate your value using your résumé. When you are an employee, you can communicate your value using submissions to your personnel file. Do you know what's in your personnel file? What can you add to it? When you are the provider of products or services, you can communicate value using a product sheet or a service proposal. When we are asking for support, such as guidance, directions, advice, or connections, we can communicate our value instantly by sharing with the other person our passion and conviction underlying our beat-the-alarm goals and our commitment to achieving them. Whatever its form, you want to ensure that your communication argues your value on your behalf. If you've written it down, submit it to the Human Resources department at your company to be placed in your personnel file, hand it to the interviewer or your boss, or send it to your potential customer. In unstructured conversations, communicate your value by starting your "ask" with some statement that informs the other party of your contributions and your potential. Regardless of the situation, guarantee the other party knows your value by first knowing it yourself and then communicating it on paper, in conversation, or by offering an experience of it.

Colonel Sanders, founder of Kentucky Fried Chicken, knew better than anyone the importance of communicating value. After perfecting his secret "finger-lickin' good" recipe, the Colonel traveled across the country in his car communicating the value of the recipe to chefs everywhere by offering them free tastes. He then asked them to sell his chicken in their restaurants. He heard "No" many times. Some chefs didn't even want to taste his recipe; others didn't want to sell it in spite of its unique flavor. The Colonel kept knocking on doors and sharing the irresistible chicken, until he started hearing "Yes." It is estimated that by the time he was 60, the Colonel had accumulated over a thousand "Nos." His methodology was atypical, especially in the 1950s, but the Colonel knew that he had created something special. With that conviction, he kept sharing and asking, thus beginning the journey that resulted in one of the largest fast food chains in existence.

My own fear of rejection halted me from asking for more during a job interview once, and a year into the position, I kicked myself for the thousands of dollars of salary I lost. I was interviewing for a position that was clearly bigger than my experience, and because I did not "act as if" I had the right to interview for this position, the company was not convinced that I was the right person for the job. I was completely unclear as to my own value and the value that I brought to them. As a result, they offered me a lesser title and salary, and I took it without asking for more. A year into the job, I realized what a costly mistake I had made. Not only did I settle for less money than I earned at my last job, but I hadn't asked for a signing bonus, which apparently all other high-level employees had asked for and received. I worked extremely hard, and I clearly earned a greater salary, let alone a bigger title. I was frustrated and mad that no one from the executive team had noticed, and I all I could do was blame myself for not knowing my value, communicating it, and asking for more.

Brooke, a very talented architect, similarly lost a lot of money and self-respect because she did not know her own value and had no skills to communicate it. She was trained in architect design in Europe; however, because she did not have a certification from a U.S. accredited university, she could not officially call herself an architect in the U.S. This tainted her value in her own mind in spite of her extremely rare talent in designing homes. When several friends asked her to design their homes, she did. But because she did not comprehend her own worth, she didn't charge any of them for her talented services. She provided enormous value, but she was blind to it. Finally fed up, she went to work to understand her own value. Brooke spent a few months researching what other people charge for similar design services; she documented her value, including her education, experience, and services; and she practiced various ways of communicating her value to others. Soon Brooke was holding her head high, communicating, asking, and being paid what she is worth even from the cadre of friends that she had trained to mooch from her.

ASKING POWERFULLY.

People with moxie never ask with their tail between their legs or their tongue stuck in their throat. They ask as if they will get. They ask powerfully crafted questions with vigor, confidence, and conviction. The key is in the way that they ask, the words they use, and the confidence their body language exudes. Each contributes to the others.

Asking powerfully requires first that we ask powerful questions. These are open-ended questions that elicit conversation and feedback. Powerful questions do not allow for a yes or no answer. Notice the difference between: "Can I have more money?" and "What will it take to get my salary increased?" or "Do you want to purchase the product?" and "What can we do to move forward?" or "Can you help me?" and "I could use your support." Open-ended questions will generate answers that provide information to help you move in one direction or another. Conversely, yes and no are static. So ask questions that generate answers you can use. For example, "What interests you about my product or service?" or "What can we do to make a deal?" or "When can we get started?"

The most powerful question is "What will it take...?" This is a great question that conjures an image of you moving yourself to the other side of the table to sit next to the person you are asking, and creating instant team mentality. The what-will-it-take question is ideal when talking about business: "What will it take for us to do business together?" When negotiating housework with your family: "What will it take for you to clean the house this weekend?" And when interviewing for a job: "Once I start working, what will it take for me to get promoted to the next level and receive a raise?" The instant the other person answers, the blindfold is removed. You know what it will take, and you can move in that direction or choose another one.

I used this approach to reclaim the salary I lost when I didn't know my value, I didn't act *as if*, and as a result I didn't ask. I drafted a three-page memo detailing all of my accomplishments and contributions to the company since I started working there along with salary surveys documenting the fair market value for my position. With my heart pounding in my chest screaming its fears to me, I walked into my boss' office and made a case for an increase in my salary. I asked powerfully this time. My question to him was not, "Can I have a raise?" It was "What do we need to do to get my salary increased?" After much conversation, he shared with me about the company's salary freeze and his inability to increase my salary. So together we brainstormed and decided on an immediate bonus to make up for last year's shortfall in my salary and a guaranteed bonus for the current year. Not using my moxie cost me at the onset. When I eventually became resentful and finally cognizant of my value, I was able to communicate it in a powerful ask, create a team approach with my boss, and get the money I wanted, even if it wasn't in the way that I had originally anticipated.

Powerfully crafted questions are only as powerful as the way you ask them. First, formulate the questions on a piece of paper, and then practice them out loud until they flow smoothly from your lips. You don't have to act as if you know everything already; you only need to act as if you have the right to ask your question. Don't apologize for asking. Apologize only for things that you have done wrong. Don't ever be sorry for asking for something you need. When you act as if you are sorry, people think as if you are sorry. As part of practicing the question, practice the *ask*. Use your act-as-if body language tools to exude confidence. How are you standing? What is your voice doing? Where are your eyes? How tall do you feel?

As you read the following question, imagine asking it with a high-pitched nervous voice, eye contact on the floor, a forced smile, slumped shoulders, and a hesitant stance. "I'm sorry for disturbing you. I know this may seem like a dumb question, but I was hoping that I might bother you for a favor. I need help with a project, but you are probably busy, and I shouldn't have asked you. But if you aren't, maybe you can come on Saturday morning?" Compare that to the following, and now imagine asking with a strong voice, a tall posture, a confident facial expression, square shoulders, and direct eye contact: "When you have a moment I need to talk with you about this amazing project of mine. This one pager gives you more information on its enormous value to the community. As you can see, I need people like you to help me make it successful with donations of time and money. In what way can I count on your support?" Notice the difference in not only the words you choose but your body language and, as a result, your confidence.

Stop Talking.

If you are not feeling confident, the moment after the *ask* is the moment to start acting as if you do. Silence makes us uncomfortable, but with the silence comes power. The silence screams the confidence we feel in our right to ask. Instead, most of us tend to fill that silence with too much talking, especially when we really need something and even more so when we are nervous about asking for someone to help us with that need. Women tend to do more of this nervous air-filling than men. Their relationships are more interdependent and therefore they worry about the impact of their *ask* on the other person. Their post-ask talking is an expression of that concern. Men, on the other hand, assume that the other party in the *ask* will take care of themselves and will let us know if they have an objection or concern.

As a result of filling the air with unnecessary talking, we risk missing out on valuable information that the other person would have shared but for being distracted by our nervous chattering. For example, sometimes we ask our powerful question, but then follow it up with a bunch of apologies and justifications for asking, essentially destroying any power our question once had. It often sounds something like this: "I need to add someone to my team. What do we need to do to put this headcount in the budget this quarter? But it might be a dumb request in light of our cost-cutting, and this is probably not a good time. I could come back later. You're probably under a lot of stress, huh? I know I can really do a great job here, and I know that adding a person to the team will allow us to move forward. We are strong, but maybe we just need to work harder ourselves, but I'm sure we could be stronger if only we had a few more people..." Stop! Only when we *stop talking* after we ask can we hear the response, and only then can we respond to any objections. Stop talking after you ask, and you show your confidence in the silence that ensues.

CHECKING IN.

In some situations it is more productive to ask a lot of conversational checking-in questions before jumping in to the one big, powerful question. Imagine testing the ice on a frozen pond before stepping on it. If your toe goes through the ice, you need to find a more solid place on which to tread. For example, imagine meeting with a new customer and explaining to him about the services you offer. If you immediately followed the presentation with, "What will it take to do business together?" your customer might shut down your ask immediately because he does not understand the value of your service. He could be stuck back at the beginning of the presentation where you explain how your services work. Frustrated and confused, it would be very easy for him to say "No." Instead of risking that, check in along the route and get the opportunity to overcome mini-objections as they arise. Checking in along the way is helpful in the process because it allows you to garner agreement as you go. This will also make the bigger *ask* that much easier.

Unlike the *ask*, checking in is the perfect time to use yes-and-no questions, because you are seeking a lot of little easy agreements. In the situation with the new customer, you could ask a series of questions along the way, such as "Do you understand how this service works?" "Do you see how it could eliminate cost overruns in your manufacturing team?" "Do you agree that saving money while ensuring the quality of your product is a top priority for you?" Once you collect the string of 'Yeses,' you can confidently ask for the business. If the customer disagrees at any point, you have the opportunity to clarify and move towards agreement. You can use the checking-in technique when discussing salary, negotiating housework, asking for support, or even asking someone to marry you!

Salvage the No.

When you add the strategy called *ask*, you are vulnerable to another person's power to say "No." People with moxie are never stopped by the word *No* – their resolve is merely tested by it. With a little pre-work before the *ask*, you will be in a position to respond, address their concerns, and resuscitate the potential of a "Yes."

Pre-work includes anticipating possible objections and preparing responses. When you consider asking someone for a raise, a contract, a job, or even a date, think about the objections that will surface. Craft responses to those anticipated objections before you ask and hold them in reserve. When the objection is presented, restate their objection to ensure you have heard clearly and understand it. Then respond directly and address their concerns. For example, if you are seeking a raise and you anticipate the response will be "We have no budget for a raise," your response might be "I understand the company is in a budget crunch and concerned about additional expenses. If I generate an additional $500,000 in revenue in the next three months with my brilliant new idea, we could apply a portion of this revenue to my salary without impacting the company's bottom line." If you are seeking to close a contract with a new customer and you anticipate an objection such as "Your service costs too much," your response could be "I understand that the cost of our service feels a little uncomfortable to you. If I could save your company $500,000 with our new solution, would it be worth the fraction of savings that it cost you for the service?" If you have asked someone out on a date and the response is, "I'm seeing someone," your moxie response could be "I understand you are already in a relationship. Keep in mind that I would treat you like a queen. When you are no longer seeing someone else, please do let me know."

MARKET RESEARCH.

A "No" is always an opportunity to garner market research. Even when the "No" does not come with an objection, you have the ability to ask follow-up questions to elicit the reasons behind it and collect your market research. When you are responding, there are two critical questions to have in your arsenal at all times: "What is your concern?" and "What will it take for you to say "Yes?" What better way to find out what their objection is? With that information, you can respond accordingly. They might say "I'm concerned that the product won't work," to which you could respond with a product demo or a sample product to test. Or they may express a concern that you won't deliver on time, to which you could guarantee them an on-time delivery or a full refund. What great market research! This is an opportunity to discover others' perceptions of you or your products or services. Companies pay large amounts of money in focus groups to obtain this kind of information. Be grateful; don't be defensive.

Often we cannot anticipate an objection. The best response in these situations is to throw up the negotiations flag with, "What can we do to make it work?" or "What will it take?" From here the other person begins to reveal what is important to them. You will quickly learn the key that could turn the objection into a "Yes" or even a step in that direction. For example, as you are negotiating with your family regarding the division of household chores, you may hear from your spouse, "I am horrible at doing dishes, and I hate doing them." You could respond, "Let's brainstorm! You agree that it takes both of us to make this house run smoothly, correct? What will it take for you to do the dishes? What can we do to make this work?" From here, the negotiations are open. Your spouse may offer to do something that you hate doing, like cleaning the bathroom, in exchange for not doing the dishes.

If your children are negotiating with you for an allowance or a curfew, teach them a similar approach. Show them that your "No" is just a curtain behind which lie your concerns for their safety and responsibility. Teach them that if they start asking questions such as "What are your concerns?" and "What will it take for me to earn a dollar more in my allowance?" or "What will it take for you to allow me to stay out past 10:00 PM?" then you will meet them halfway at the negotiations table. Suddenly, instead of an antagonistic and heated conversation that rips at your relationships, you are now brainstorming together to meet everyone's wants and address everyone's concerns.

With one foot out the door at my second law firm job, I created a moxie moment with an *ask* that to this day I wear like a medal around my neck. It was my last day at the firm before leaving to become an attorney for one of my clients. I was a corporate transaction attorney and upon giving notice, my many deals were reassigned to other attorneys at the firm, except for one. Mary Beth from the Human Resources department walked into my office and made me an offer to complete the last transaction as a contract attorney after my departure. She said the firm was willing to pay me $60 an hour. I thanked her for the offer and said that I would think about it. Sixty dollars is not an insignificant amount, but I knew they were billing me out at $250 an hour. I also was not notably fond of my experience at this firm, so I didn't feel compelled to jump at the offer to help them.

After she left my office, I marched down the hall to the managing partner's office and knocked on his door acting *as if*. At his growl, I entered and said, "I just spoke with Mary Beth. I understand that you would like me to finish up that last transaction on a contract basis after I leave and that you're willing to pay me $60 an hour." I paused and looked him straight in the eye with all the moxie I could muster and said, "I want 200." Flabbergasted, he growled again and said, "200?! We've never paid 200, and we're not going to pay it now." With this objection, I responded, "You bill me out at $250 an hour, and after I leave you won't be paying any overhead for me, so the $50 difference will be gravy in your pocket." I took another breath and said, "I want 200." And then I stopped talking. I was pretty sure the pounding of my heart was loud enough to fill any silence that ensued. He looked at me, growled again, turned back to his computer, and in a sweep of defeat, said, "Fine." I walked down the hall in celebration and recounted my coup with every attorney on the floor. In the one month that it took for me to complete that last transaction, I made an additional $10,000.

The important moxie lesson here is that I asked and asked powerfully. I acted as if I had the right to ask, I asked, I responded to the objections, and I didn't fill the silence with unnecessary words. I had many choices in this situation. I could have thanked Mary Beth and said "No way." I could have accepted her offer and made some additional money, although it would have been less than what I did ultimately earn. I could have asked for an even higher or lower amount than I did. The partner's response could have varied as well. He could have said "Absolutely not" or he could have countered with another number. There was also the chance that the *ask* would have gotten me nowhere and that $60 was their highest offer. Regardless of the outcome, I asked, and I did it with moxie.

Practice.

Being powerful at asking takes practice. Begin by practicing in the mirror or with your friends or family. And then find opportunities to practice in less uncomfortable situations. Recall that we find asking difficult because too often we are concerned with what others think of us. So find situations to practice in which you do not know the other person. For instance, call your credit card company and practice your *ask* with the account representative. To them you are merely a number. They don't know you personally. They won't recognize you at the grocery store. Ask them for a lower interest rate. With a powerful, confident voice, say "I have been a great customer of yours in spite of many opportunities to work with other credit card companies that promise lower interest rates. I would like the interest rate on my card decreased to a lower amount. What's the best rate you can offer me?" After this, be quiet and allow them to answer. If they say "No," ask, "What will it take to lower my interest rate?" If they say "Yes," go one step further and ask them what it would take to lower it even further.

When you phrase your question in this way, they will likely reveal to you what it will take to lower the interest rate on your credit card. They may share with you that in six months you'll be eligible for a decrease in your interest rate, or that if you eliminate some debt, your credit score will go up which will allow them to lower your interest rate. Remember, you are not being obnoxious. You are asking for what you need, which is more money in your pocket, not theirs. Their answers will provide you with valuable information that you can use to move forward. Also remember that you never know unless you ask. You could be paying more interest than you need to be paying, and it is not likely that they'll call and let you know that you are paying too much. Finally remember that the credit card company will take care of itself. They want your business and don't want you to leave. Don't be concerned that you are impacting their business by asking for a lower interest rate. They know exactly how low they can go. But somewhere in between hurting their bottom line and hurting yours is some middle ground that is up for grabs. Start grabbing.

Feed the Meter.

Regardless of your powerful questions, the amount of practice, or the anticipated objections, situations will inevitably arise that take unpredictable turns. When the conversation goes sideways and takes us with it, regrouping, even momentarily, is essential. When you face the hostility of a "bully," stepping away from the conversation is your greatest ally. When you are presented with new facts that twist your assumptions, you need an opportunity to think clearly. In all of these situations, we need to walk away, remember our value, strategize a new approach, and think of alternative responses. You could ask to use the washroom, make a quick phone call, or feed a parking meter. Whatever your reason, you need to extract yourself from the aggression or challenge that is getting in the way of asking for something you want or need. For example, "Would you excuse me for a moment, I need to use the washroom." or "Please excuse me, I need to a make a quick phone call." or "Do you have a tissue?" Say anything! Just distract the heat from this conversation.

One LifeMoxie! client successfully used this strategy to regroup after negotiations went sideways on her. Dana was presenting a proposal for her program to the executive director of a non-profit. The director quickly saw the possibilities of the program and couldn't wait to get started. Her comments, however, indicated her assumption that Dana was not going to charge for her services. Thrown off, Dana didn't know what to do next. Her business model was based on being paid for her program, even from non-profit organizations. Dana excused herself from the table with the excuse of needing to put a quarter in the parking meter and walked outside for a few minutes. She needed this opportunity to think of what to say next to let the director know that this program was going to cost money; however, she didn't want to burst the director's excitement for Dana and the program with a heavy conversation about money. With a new approach,

Dana returned to the table at the restaurant and said, "As we can both see, this program will be a great solution for your organization. Let's talk about your budget." Feeding the meter gave Dana the opportunity to regroup and shift the conversation in a professional, yet direct manner. While the director was momentarily stunned by the turn of the conversation, the clear and confident shift allowed her to shift her thinking to money. As a result Dana delivered a great program to the non-profit, and the director compensated her fairly.

THE BACK-UP PLAN.

At the end of it all, you may not be able to salvage the "No," in which case you need a back-up plan. Going in at the beginning of an *ask* with a back-up plan will give you the most power because you will not be dependent on the other person to achieve your beat-the-alarm goals. The other party will be just one avenue; they are not your only solution. When you have an alternative route available, you are no longer vulnerable to the whims of the other person. You have options. Having a back-up plan allows you to respond not just react.

As long as we never relinquish to another person or any circumstance the power over our ability to move forward, the "what ifs" are meaningless. We need to ask, but we also need to know that if they say "No," we have other options. When we know our worst-case scenario, the person being asked never has complete control over our success or happiness.

HOW TO USE THIS STRATEGY TO CREATE MOXIE.

What beat-the-alarm goals are you working on? Each day you need something from someone else to accomplish those goals. You need time, support, money, connections, or assistance from others. If you don't ask, people won't instantly know how to contribute to you or your beat-the-alarm goals. When you do ask, do so with moxie. Be confident, act as if you have the right to ask, remember your alternatives, and be ready to learn new information that will drive you closer to your beat-the-alarm goals, with or without the *Yes!* to your ask.

Exercises to Ask

- What is your biggest fear about asking?

- What is the hardest thing to ask for?

- Write a powerful *ask* statement for that.

- Anticipate the objections to your *ask* and write a few responses.

- Think of a back-up plan.

- Practice your *ask* in the mirror and practice adding silence after you ask.

- Practice by asking powerfully for smaller things, such as the cost of a product or for directions.

- Call your credit card company and ask for a lower interest rate.

- In a tough situation, employ a feed the meter excuse, such as needing to make a call or find the washroom.

Be Uncomfortable

. . . .

Choosing Your Mission
over Your Comfort

Being uncomfortable is the one feeling that most of us work our whole lives to avoid. Unfortunately, however, in that quest we end up avoiding the world of experiences that accompany those uncomfortable feelings. Routine results in mediocrity, while risk results in excellence. Moxie starves in the comfort zone, so consider comfort the nemesis of moxie. Moxie requires that we act *as if and* be uncomfortable at the same time. Only then do we really push through to greatness. We avoid discomfort because of our fears of adventuring outside our comfort zone. However, as soon as we shift the focus back to our beat-the-alarm goals and our past successes in uncomfortable situations, staying put will soon become the new discomfort that we work to avoid.

In 1955, Rosa Parks exchanged her comfort for her beat-the-alarm goal as she refused to relinquish her seat to a white passenger on a bus in Montgomery, Alabama. Ms. Parks was a seamstress who rode the bus to work and a civil rights activist who worked behind the scenes to end racial segregation. The first four rows of seats on all the buses at that time were reserved for white people; the "colored" sections in the back of the bus were for black people. On December 1, 1955, Ms. Parks was sitting in the front of the "colored" section when the bus driver ordered her and other blacks to move back a few rows to accommodate the extra white people who were standing without any available seats in the white section. Ms. Parks recalls the moment as one in which a determination came over her like a blanket. Suddenly being uncomfortable became a small price to pay to further her mission. She recalls that she was 42 and tired of giving in. She refused to give up her seat and was subsequently arrested and charged with disorderly conduct. Rosa Parks' moment of being uncomfortable triggered the Montgomery Bus Boycott four days later on December 5, 1955, history's largest and most successful mass movement against racial segregation. And, as a result of her choosing her beat-the-alarm goal over her comfort, the boycott catapulted one of its organizers to the forefront of the civil rights movement, Dr. Martin Luther King, Jr.

COMFORT ZONE.

We love the comfort zone. We know what to do here. We know what to expect; we know what is expected of us. There are no surprises. We hate to be bothered, feel unsure, or put in situations that could cause us embarrassment. We would much rather be comfortable, so we often choose it over our commitments. When we even think of venturing outside of this zone, we experience a variety of physical manifestations of that unwillingness to be uncomfortable: heart palpitations, excessive talking, incessant giggling, nausea, or even hives.

Why do we embrace this zone and sometimes even apply a death grip to it? The answer can be found in our fears: fear of the unknown, fear of consequences, fear of rejection, and fear of scarcity, all prompted by a lifetime of evidence that we've gathered proving that adventuring outside the comfort zone is dangerous. These fears cause us to engage in irrational behavior, accept unreasonable circumstances, make ridiculous statements, and choose foolishly. All in the name of being comfortable. And even if you believe that your behavior, circumstances, statements, and choices are rational and reasonable, the fact that you are not pursuing your beat-the-alarm goals or prioritizing your life could be considered in and of itself irrational, unreasonable, ridiculous, and foolish.

Raymond's family is not used to expressing their feelings to each other. After so many years, Raymond feels too uncomfortable to share with his children how much he appreciates and loves them. He has spent a lifetime showing them his love in different ways, and he thinks this is enough. Raymond clings to his comfort zone, as that is what he has known his whole life. He is afraid of what might happen if he does say the actual words to his family. He has no idea how they would react, if they would reciprocate the feelings, or if they would laugh at him uncomfortably. He is too afraid to find out, and his children are also too uncomfortable to ask. These words remain unspoken among Raymond's family.

In the movie *Joe vs. the Volcano*, Joe feels physically stuck in the comfort zone of his life and becomes free only when diagnosed with a terminal illness. The movie opens to a scene where Joe and a thousand other downtrodden workers, all dressed in grey trench coats, are trudging to a factory to the tune of a song about owing their soul to the company. Their energy-sucking office – from the buzzing, fluorescent lighting to the dark halls and eerie silence to the erratic boss who shouts "Nobody feels great, Joe. After childhood it's a fact of life." – adds to the misery Joe feels physically and emotionally in his flat-lined existence. Despondent, lost, and demoralized, nothing excites him about his life. After insisting for additional tests, the doctor informs Joe that he has six months to live as a result of a terminal brain cloud. This diagnosis breaks the chains for Joe. Suddenly he feels more alive than ever before. He returns to the office to quit his job and tell his boss what he thinks. "In the beginning I was full of piss and vinegar. I don't know what happened. But I became chicken-shit. Afraid to live my life, so I sold it to you for $300 a week! No more." Approached with an offer to live like a king and die like a man by sacrificing his life to a volcano, Joe agrees. He is driven by this last beat-the-alarm goal — to give his life some meaning that it had lost. In his journey, he falls in love with himself, with a woman, and with the possibility of his life. Like Joe, most people need a death sentence to free them physically and emotionally from their comfort zone.

Fear of the Unknown.

The devil we know is better than the devil we don't. As a result, most people stay in jobs, relationships, and situations long after they know they should leave. What would happen if they ventured out from the world they know? Would they survive? Would it be a horrible experience? What if they fail? What if they're embarrassed? What if it's just more of the same? What if the unknown results in even more misery? Not willing to take a chance, they cling to their comfort zone. The fear of the unknown causes people everywhere to numb themselves with anti-depressants, pain-killers, alcohol, drugs, cigarettes, and food, and other destructive behaviors instead of changing their lives.

Most people resist changing even those aspects of their lives they don't like because they have learned to survive the lives they created. They might be miserable currently, but at least they've learned how to manage their miserable situation. They have no idea what awaits them, but they know that changing their life to discover it will test their ability to survive again. Joanne has stayed married to her drug-addicted, cheating, gambling husband for 30 years because she fears the unknown more than she fears living the rest of her life with this man. She has managed to survive this life that she knows, and she does not want to learn how to survive a new one. Rebecca, on the other hand, has been battling her leukemia for 10 years and wants to study abroad. Her fear of not experiencing the world before she dies is greater than her fear of the unknown, so she will do whatever it takes to get herself into a study-abroad program to see the world.

Larry has held the same government job for the past 25 years, since college. He is well paid, he knows what to expect, and he knows the people, and the people know him. Even though he is unfulfilled, there is no compelling reason to change jobs. His fear of the unknown outweighs his craving for fulfillment. What if he left the comfort of his current situation in search of fulfillment, and he didn't know where to look, or worse yet, never found it? What if the grass only seems greener from this side? At least in his current situation he's got it all figured out – there are no surprises. The fear of the unknown has Larry clinging to the comfort of his job. When the pain of staying where he is becomes greater than the pain of not seeking out fulfillment, Larry will leave his job even if he has no idea where he is headed. Until then count on Larry staying put.

The story of the jumping fleas exemplifies our resistance to venturing out from the world we know. When jumping fleas are placed in a jar with a lid to stop them from jumping out, they jump to the top and hit the lid. Soon they learn that they can only jump as high as the lid on the jar. When the lid is removed, these critters still won't jump any higher than the top of the jar because they have conditioned themselves to believe that the lid will stop them. This is often how we run our lives. We stop ourselves by the lid we *believe* is above us. We don't even try to go beyond the "lid." We tried once, and it failed, so we "know" that we will get stopped again. Why even try?

Let's imagine a different approach. We know what this life looks like, and we can always come back to it. We have no idea what is waiting for us out there. What if it is wonderful? What if it is not what we expected at all? What if it is everything we wanted and then some? If it's horrible, we can always come back to this life. Success or failure – either way we will learn something about ourselves, we will learn something about life, and we will have an adventure. That alone is priceless.

Frank followed this approach, leaving his full-time dental practice to create a speaking business based on an innovative game he created to help people make money. His success was not only not guaranteed, but it was not an easy road to travel. Frank encountered many failures along the way, but unlike most people, he took a chance by stepping outside his comfort zone in favor of what he defined as a more fulfilling and lucrative career. As a result, he was rewarded with opportunities, adventure, and fulfillment.

We can always tell when we cling to our comfort zone as a result of a fear of the unknown because we become riddled with excuses as to why we cannot move forward. Sandi had spent many years in the seminary studying to become a minister, and she needed only an apprenticeship to complete her studies. This, however, was not an easy task. To obtain an apprenticeship, Sandi had to apply to churches all over the country, interview, and move away from home for 10 months. She proceeded to muddle the next four years of her life with excuses about why she couldn't complete her seminary training. She didn't have enough money to move; she didn't know how her husband and daughter would handle things without her; she didn't have enough time to apply for an apprenticeship and work out the details. Beneath all of those excuses lay Sandi's fear of the unknown. What if no parish wanted her? What if she didn't like the parish if one did actually accept her? What if she wasn't very good at being a minister? What if she failed completely?

After years had passed Sandi started thinking about the experience she was missing and her beat-the-alarm goal she had pushed aside. She realized that she could always come back to the life that she had known. And she admitted that her husband and grown daughter would manage just fine without her for a few months. With this new approach she moved forward on her beat-the-alarm goal in the face of all those fears. She applied to parishes all over the country, left her job, and moved 3,000 miles away from home to complete the journey she had started eight years earlier. The moment she began to fear missing out on the experience and accomplishing her beat-the-alarm goal, she moved forward in spite of these fears. Sandi eliminated each of her excuses, embraced the uncomfortable, and was awarded with a life-changing experience.

Fear of Consequences.

Before taking any new step, we sometimes over-analyze our situation, attempting to play through in our minds all possible results and consequences. Similar to the limited benefit of the "what ifs" that race through our head before an *ask,* there is limited benefit in the over-analysis. The analysis is processed entirely in our heads, while the consequences are played out in reality with other people and their unpredictable behaviors. As a result, our analysis and the actual consequences are rarely the same.

Consequences that we fear often include being judged or ridiculed by others, losing money, losing friends, being punished, or enduring harm physically or emotionally. For example, public speaking brings with it the fear of looking like a fool in front of a crowd. This fear of being ridiculed causes most people to fear public speaking even more than they fear death. Again, however, when your beat-the-alarm goals are so compelling, you will push those fears aside in favor of pushing your beat-the-alarm goals forward.

The fear of particular consequences can cause our comfort zone to shrink. When younger children touch a hot stove, they get burned both physically and emotionally and carry these consequences with them forever. Recalling these fears, they steer clear of the stove for fear of being burned again. Unfortunately, too often we use past wounds to paralyze us in the face of identified future dangers. These memories of being wounded create walls around us that, as the years go by and the hurts pile up, close in on us. As a result, our comfort zone gets smaller and smaller. Suddenly we don't want to make any move based on the hot stove we touched when we were 7. Consider Elaine's hot stove story. When she was growing up she entered a baton-twirling contest only to come in last place. Her dad yelled at her in front of her friends for wasting the family's time on something so silly. "At least you could have tried harder!" he said. This experience scarred Elaine and shrunk her comfort zone. She carried this fear of touching a hot stove with her into her adult life and never again tried anything new in which success was not guaranteed.

Peer pressures that teenagers face from their purported friends about alcohol or drugs are fueled by this fear of consequences. Their reputations, social status, and friendships are at stake if they don't participate in the "experiment" or join the fun. The social consequences of not going along with their friends often weigh so heavily on them that they don't feel like they have a choice. However, they will not succumb to this peer pressure if their fear of punishment from their parents or even the law is greater than the fear of being ridiculed or losing friends.

The other salvation teenagers have from this peer pressure is a beat-the-alarm goal. When teenagers are intentionally working towards their future, it will be easier for them to rebuff the pressure to be cool in the present. They will risk embarrassment and justify it with a conviction that they are working on their future. For instance, a student who dreams of going to college and becoming an FBI agent does not want to do anything in the present that would jeopardize that beat-the-alarm goal. Or a student who wants to go to medical school will not sabotage his success for a night of partying with drugs. When teenagers are clear about their future and operate from their beat-the-alarm goals, they will be less likely to surrender to social pressures and the accompanying consequences. Our job as adults is to give them the tools to articulate missions and set goals, the confidence to operate from them, and the moxie to do so. With those tools, that confidence, and the moxie, they will be equipped to move forward in the direction of their beat-the-alarm goals regardless of feeling uncomfortable in the moment of peer pressure.

FEAR OF REJECTION.

The fear of rejection is one of those consequences that we fear more than most. No one likes to be rejected. In fact, we work most of our lives to avoid being rejected. We want people to like us. Sally Field summed up this lifelong quest for all of us when she accepted her second Oscar in 1985 and shouted with glee "I can't deny the fact that you like me, right now, you like me!" Being rejected is extremely uncomfortable and as a result, we avoid it.

Unfortunately, the fear of rejection also makes finding a life partner more challenging. Dating is not for the faint at heart due to the vulnerability it demands of its participants, and blind dates and on-line dating require another level of vulnerability altogether. Many single hearts avoid dating because while they want a life partner, they don't want to risk rejection. So they choose their comfortable life rather than endure the possibility of being uncomfortable. They fear disappointment and the hurt feelings of a broken heart. The dating ritual is reserved for people who are willing to risk those feelings and to be uncomfortable in the short term for the beat-the-alarm goal of finding a soul mate in the long term. When finding a life partner becomes more important than the risk of disappointment, rejection, or a broken heart, single hearts will jump in.

Likewise, the vulnerability that accompanies the words "I love you" leaves our heart open and at risk of getting hurt, so we avoid being the first to say it. But, when our commitment to keep the one we love is stronger than our commitment to our own comfort, the words will start rolling from our lips.

Fear of Scarcity.

Scarcity is often the fuel behind our death grip on comfort. We cling to our money, our ideas, our possessions, and even our friends. We are convinced that there is only so much to go around. In our comfort zone, we know exactly what we have and exactly what we don't have. If we were to venture outside the comfort zone, what we do have might be taken from us. We lose sight of the fact that we might gain more than we might lose if we were to risk the journey.

Rock band Pearl Jam in 1994 did not let a scarcity mentality reign over their personal commitment to their fans. They were outraged by the exorbitant fees that Ticketmaster was charging Pearl Jam fans to attend their concerts. In a scarcity mentality, Pearl Jam could have overlooked this and focused on the money that the band was making. If they had operated out of scarcity, they would have chosen the comfort of guaranteed money, and they would have disregarded their feelings or convictions about the situation. Instead Pearl Jam chose an uncomfortable situation, using alternative ticketing companies and non-Ticketmaster venues. This was a huge risk that put their concert tour as well as their revenue in jeopardy. Their commitment to their fans, however, was a mission of the band that prevailed over their comfort zone. As a result, Pearl Jam was rewarded for their commitment; their shows were wildly successful thereby solidifying the loyalty of their fans.

Consequences of the Comfort Zone.

When we cling to our comfort zone we miss out on a world of experiences, learnings, and brilliance. We get stuck in routine, and in routine there is no oxygen for moxie. The good news about your comfort zone is that you know exactly what your life will present to you. The bad news is that you are guaranteed a good if not mediocre life, not a great one. Who strives for a life of mediocrity? We all hunger for greatness. But only goodness lives in the comfort zone; the comfort zone knows no greatness. Only when we are focused on our beat-the-alarm goals and our missions will we choose to be uncomfortable instead of dictated by our fears. As we begin driving towards our missions, we need to celebrate our uncomfortable inventory, recruit a cheerleading squad to come along for the uncomfortable ride, take on challenges, think big, and act collaboratively.

Sometimes the greatest gift comes when we are involuntarily booted from our comfort zone. For instance, when we get fired from a job, we don't have the luxury of deciding if we are ready to let go of our familiar and predictable routine in search of a more fulfilling career. We are forced into the unknown. Quite often this boot is a gift that in the moment just feels like an injustice. If you are fired from your job or served divorce papers, consider it the catapult you need to get out of your comfort zone. From here you can explore your options, discover your missions, and create your beat-the-alarm goals, or you can quickly find a replacement job or spouse without doing any work whatsoever to determine what made you unhappy in the first place. You will either make the same mistakes by jumping quickly into another job or marriage that looks like your first one, or you'll spend time figuring out what you want in a career or a relationship. Either way, the choice is yours to immediately recreate a comfort zone or to embrace the uncomfortable in favor of your own greatness.

Being Uncomfortable for a Mission.

Every uncomfortable act has some underlying mission, and it's usually a compelling mission that propels us from our comfort zone. If there is any reason to be uncomfortable, it is for something greater than the comfort of our couch. Even daredevils who seem to do wildly crazy and insane acts for no reason (in spite of their inevitable fear of getting hurt) do so out of some compelling mission, like fame or fortune. You will forgo your own comfort when you become clear about your missions and start working on the beat-the-alarm goals that will further those missions.

Gandhi's compelling mission was peace in India. Nelson Mandela's compelling mission was freedom from apartheid. Mother Teresa's compelling mission was ending poverty and hunger around the world. Elizabeth Cady Stanton's compelling mission was women's suffrage. (Even her compatriot Lucretia Mott feared the inevitable societal ridicule from demanding the vote for women that Ms. Stanton wrote into the Declaration of Sentiments in 1848.) Each of these individuals risked their reputations, their money, their homes, their futures, and their lives. Each of these individuals was driven by a deep and passionate mission, without which they too would have clung to their own comfort zones.

Our comfort zone thrives in small thinking. We wonder how we could impact our lives, let alone the world. The practice of thinking big leaves no room for being comfortable; in fact, it thrives in being uncomfortable. Mother Teresa was a frail woman and a big thinker. She dedicated her life to the elimination of poverty regardless of the plethora of evidence that she would not be successful. Aware of the likelihood that she would not see the elimination of poverty in her lifetime, she drove in that direction regardless. She disregarded her own fears, others' judgments, and the predisposed failure that she faced. She chose her mission over the comfort of an easy life with easily achievable goals. Mother Teresa's moxie made an impact on the world and defined her legacy. In what ways do you think small and sacrifice opportunities to make a bigger impact?

Mahatma Gandhi was another big thinker who chose a mission over the easy comfortable life. At the insistence of his family, he began his life as a British-educated lawyer, and as such could have lived a very comfortable life practicing law. But it was in South Africa that he discovered his passion for fighting the injustices levied against Indians. Influenced by his upbringing, one of his missions was non-injury to living beings, and one of his life's beat-the-alarm goals was the non-violent independence of India from foreign domination. Suddenly, he wanted more than a comfortable life. He employed his inspiration for peaceful civil disobedience in even the most extreme situations. Gandhi, a student of Hindu philosophy, led a simple life, but his big thinking changed a nation.

Nelson Mandela, also a big thinker, chose being uncomfortable to further his mission to end apartheid. While in prison, Mr. Mandela continued to further his mission in spite of his 27-year imprisonment. He knew he could not do it alone, so he worked to collaborate with the men who imprisoned him to further his mission, an extremely uncomfortable situation. He enrolled his captors in his beat-the-alarm goal by educating them on the misery and injustices of apartheid. Mr. Mandela was tested during these years, but it was his moxie that allowed him to give purpose to his otherwise unfair and unjust situation.

Even the participants on television's reality show *American Idol* are driven by a mission that compels them to leave their comfort zone. These contestants voluntarily put themselves on stage in front of America, to the amusement of the judges and the ridicule of the audience. Often they do not have a voice that justifies their entrance in the door, let alone a microphone in their hand. What they do have, though, is a passion for the stage and a goal to "make it" that drives them to risk being uncomfortable for the chance of fame. In spite of their outlandish looks, painful voices, and eccentric personalities, they are in the game. It is so easy for the rest of us to sit on the couch in the comfort of our homes mocking these men and women. While we're busy laughing, we fail to acknowledge that we are witnessing a group of people who are willing to risk so much for the chance at greatness. These are people with moxie.

Asking for money is another one of those extremely uncomfortable situations that is overcome in the face of a greater mission. Our fear around it is usually grounded in that concern we explored in LifeMoxie! Strategy #4 (*Say Yes First, Figure out the How Later*) in which we worry about others' opinions and judgments about us. What will they think of us for asking? The reality is that everyone judges us every day for every choice we make. From the children we raise, to the jobs we hold, to the clothes we wear, to the cars we drive, people are judging. But we aren't normally stopped in our tracks by others' judgments when we are clear on why we are making those choices around our kids, jobs, and cars. Similarly, when we shift our thinking from a concern over their judgments back to the reason we are asking in the first place, we regain our power and push our discomfort aside. When you focus on your beat-the-alarm goals, suddenly asking becomes just one of the tools to get you closer to them.

April's beat-the-alarm goal of going to Kenya forced her to deal with two situations that make her noticeably uncomfortable: snakes and asking for money. The sight of snakes makes her shake with fear, as does asking for money. As she was preparing to lead a team of women to Kenya, she knew they would more than likely encounter snakes or reptiles during their trip, and she knew they needed to ask for money to support the tribe they were visiting. None of her team had ever been to Kenya before, and they would be looking to her for leadership.

As part of her preparations, she was determined to deal with her fears in these uncomfortable situations. She dealt with the snakes first. She visited her neighbor who owned a python in order to make peace with the snake. She entered the room, touched the snake, and eventually held it. The whole time she was aware of being completely uncomfortable, but she was more aware of her beat-the-alarm goal to lead her team to Africa. She then worked with her team to clarify their team mission for going and their beat-the-alarm goals they were working to accomplish while there. Their goals included supporting the local orphanage and schools, funding a group of 40 women with micro-loans, and teaching these women how to start and run their own businesses. Based on these beat-the-alarm goals, they wrote letters, sent e-mails, and made phone calls to raise the money they needed. Clear about their reasons for going, they were able to speak with passion and conviction in spite of being uncomfortable. By the time they left, not only was April ready for the snakes in the path, but she and the team had raised the money they needed for their journey.

In 1912 when she discovered her passion to help women with birth control options, Margaret Sanger similarly dealt with being uncomfortable. As a nurse on New York's lower East Side, she was constantly begged by women patients for solutions to their incessant states of pregnancy. Female contraception at the time was all but illegal. As a result, women everywhere were resorting to the neighborhood $5 abortionist for freedom from their situations. Coining the term "birth control," Ms. Sanger was determined to find practical and available methods for women to control their own reproductive systems. Immediately, Ms. Sanger found herself dealing with outrage from the government and organized religion. She endured ongoing battles and uncomfortable confrontations for the remainder of her life, driven nonetheless by her determination to make birth control a fundamental right of women everywhere.

Corazon Aquino similarly was driven by her passion despite the uncomfortable situation she faced. Her husband served the Philippine government as a mayor, governor, and then senator. But he was also a critic of president Ferdinand Marcos and the government, and this resulted in his arrest and death sentence. In 1980 she accompanied him into a three-year exile in the United States. Upon returning to their country in 1983, her husband was assassinated at the airport. Over the next few years, his friends and supporters convinced Ms. Aquino, an educated but quiet and docile woman, to run for president. Overnight she was thrust into the limelight, and in spite of being completely out of her comfort zone in this position, she ran for the presidency in 1986 against Marcos. Both parties claimed victory, but it was Marcos who fled the country amidst demonstrations and military opposition, and Ms. Aquino took office. Any distress, anxiety, and worry she felt in her situation was outweighed by her resolve to carry on her husband's legacy, lead her country, and end the corruption that plagued it.

UNCOMFORTABLE INVENTORY.

Just like your Accomplishments Inventory and your Survival Inventory, your Uncomfortable Inventory offers you evidence that you did it before, so you can do it again. Think of a situation where you felt uncomfortable the first time you tried something. Isn't it easier to imagine doing it again since you actually did it once and survived? The trepidation builds up in our minds and, once we survive it, it no longer feels so scary or insurmountable.

From buying your first house, to getting married, to having children, we take on these uncomfortable situations all the time. We just don't categorize them as such because we are so focused on the closing, the wedding, and the new baby. We are so committed to these beat-the-alarm goals that we become oblivious to the fact that we have ventured outside our comfort zone. Look at your life and make a list of the different situations in which you plowed ahead in spite of the uneasiness, angst, and anxiety you felt. Notice how you feel about these situations now. If they are important to you, for example, moving to a new city, changing jobs, or buying a new house, you won't feel as uncomfortable because you've done it before and you survived.

The first time I spoke on stage, I was shaking so much from fear that I could barely read the notes in front of me. I joined Toastmasters, hired a speaking coach, and forced myself to speak as much as possible. The more I put myself on stage, the more I realized I wasn't going to melt in spite of my mistakes and even embarrassing moments. The more I did it, the less I needed my notes, and the better I became. There was the day that I ventured out from behind the podium only to glance at my notes once in a while. Then one day I didn't bring any notes on stage; I just danced with the audience. Now I find it exhilarating, and I crave opportunities to do it again and again. Speaking in public is on my Uncomfortable Inventory.

Get a Cheerleading Squad.

Whenever we are attempting anything uncomfortable, it's easier to do it when we have our own cheerleading squad to support us. From running a marathon, to vacationing, to dancing in public, the barrier to entry is lowered when we have a companion. Sometimes your cheerleading squad will jump in and play; sometimes they are just on the sidelines cheering you on. Your official Yaysayers are often on the cheerleading squad. Other times it's just some crazy soul who wants to experience something new and is thrilled to have you on their cheerleading squad as well. For example, I don't know if I would have gone skydiving by myself. It helped that I was going with a group of people all of whom felt equally uncomfortable. We weren't stopped because we were doing it together. Whenever the uncomfortable stops us from moving forward, having someone along for the ride makes it so much easier to do.

Sally used a cheerleading squad to see the world. She had always dreamed of hiking in Machu Picchu but was beset with excuses – work, children, money, time, unknown territory – before she discovered that her friend had dreamt of doing the same. With a buddy by her side, Sally began doing research and found an organization that took groups to this Peruvian treasure every month. In addition, this company provided Sally and her friend with the information they needed to prepare physically and emotionally for the seven-day strenuous hike. Sally's cheerleading squad included her friend as well as the company that organized the trip. Without either, she might have clung to her excuses and missed out on the opportunity to see this part of the world.

I Dare You!

Sometimes approaching your uncomfortable situation as a challenge is the fuel that is needed to move forward. This is often a great response to Naysayers. When they tell you all the reasons it cannot be done, you can use your stubbornness as the gumption you need to make it happen. Consider it a challenge your archenemy has posed to you on the playground in grade school. Get ready to prove him wrong!

Todd and his friend were hiking down the Grand Canyon when they reached a plateau. They approached a park ranger for directions, and he said there was another four miles to go to reach the Colorado River. Since they were not planning on camping overnight, the ranger strongly suggested that the duo turn around and head back to the top. He said they would never make it down and back in one day. This challenge was the burst of energy that Todd and his friend needed. As if a dare had been placed in front of them, they began hiking intentionally and excitedly, driven by the challenge of touching the Colorado River and getting back up to the top in one day. Why? Because someone said they couldn't do it.

Sometimes our fear of missing out on an adventure will force us to forge ahead in spite of the uncomfortable situation. Lance Armstrong, seven-time winner of the Tour de France, trained for a marathon following his retirement from cycling. He has described this experience as one of the most challenging of his life. While his success on the Tour is impressive, Lance knew how to train, ride, and win – he had done it successfully seven times in a row. He had no experience running 26.2 miles. Any fear he might have felt was overshadowed by his new beat-the-alarm goal – he dared himself with the experience of this new physical challenge.

Practice Being Uncomfortable.

It takes practice to be uncomfortable. It's best to experiment with a few small, innocuous moves. Wear an outfit that's not your style and in fact will garner some stares. Sit in the front row at a lecture. Raise your hand with a question from the audience or express an unpopular opinion. Go to the movies by yourself or dine at a nice restaurant at a table for one. Go to a bar by yourself to listen to a band. Take a vacation by yourself. Sign up for karaoke oblivious of the quality of your voice. Go dancing! Notice if people stare, poke fun, or whisper with their judgments. Did you melt? Then notice that other than the spin of their opinions, nothing about your life is impacted by others' opinions, and nothing about their lives is impacted by your actions. They didn't melt either. Some people may stare in shock at your moxie, others may do so in admiration. Now imagine being uncomfortable for something you actually care about, like the accomplishment of a beat-the-alarm goal.

If you want to see people who have mastered the art of being uncomfortable, visit San Francisco, where the absurd flourishes, and the city rarely flinches. From tattoos and body piercings to purple hair and leather chaps, the people inhabiting this great city are walking self-expressions who work hard to ignore their inhibitions. The city holds a race every May called *Bay to Breakers* in which people participate wearing costumes, one outdoing the next for the seven-mile run through San Francisco. Every year without fail there is a group of older people who walk the seven miles naked, sporting only gym shoes and sunblock, seemingly oblivious to the stares, snickers, and snapping cameras. Some do it to garner the attention; some do it in spite of the attention. Either way, it takes moxie to walk naked through a crowd of people wearing nothing but a birthday suit that evidences the wear and tear of the years. Being uncomfortable does not require you to pierce your nose or walk naked through the streets of San Francisco; however it does require you to move forward in the face of the inevitable opinions and judgments that will swirl when you start taking actions around your beat-the-alarm goals.

How to Use This Strategy to Create Moxie.

Where are your comfort zones? Look at all areas of your life – relationships, job, family, friends, and hobbies – and consider which areas are stifled because you are clinging to your comfort zone. Now create your Uncomfortable Inventory – when in your life have you chosen to be uncomfortable and survived, let alone thrived? What beat-the-alarm goals were you pursuing when you chose to be uncomfortable? Practice with small, uncomfortable acts and start building your uncomfortable muscles.

Exercises to Be Uncomfortable

- Where in your life do you cling to your comfort zone?

- Create your Uncomfortable Inventory. When in your life did you forgo the comfort zone to accomplish a goal or further a mission?

- What comfort zone will you have to venture from in order to accomplish a goal or further a mission?

- Practice being uncomfortable in smaller ways by raising your hand in an audience, expressing an unpopular opinion, or wearing a bizarre and unmatched outfit in public.

STRATEGY No.

Keep Moving

· · · · · · · · · · · · · · · · ·

Making Molehills out of Mountains

Everything in life requires a first step to get started—a bicycle, an avalanche, a business, a savings plan, a tidal wave, a diet, an exercise plan, even a training program for a marathon. In order to get anywhere we have to start somewhere. There is a law in physics that says it takes more energy to get something started than to keep it going. Too often as we stare longingly up at the insurmountable mountain stacked at our feet, we wonder where we'll get the energy to even get started. When we knock those mountains down to molehills, our first step will be like skipping over a pond.

VISUALIZE.

In order to keep moving we need to know where we are going. While we spent time identifying our missions and clarifying our beat-the-alarm goals back in LifeMoxie! Strategy #1, let's start heading in that direction. Wherever you desire to go, visualize it, taste it, and feel it. What does it look like? What will you feel like when you get there, acquire it, or achieve it? Start visualizing yourself speaking from the stage to an audience of a thousand, accepting an award for your brilliant ideas, receiving a diploma for your hard-earned masters' degree, laying on the beach of your vacation, cashing your first paycheck from your new job, opening the door of your new home or retail store, meeting the person of your dreams. Psychologists everywhere contend that your subconscious mind cannot tell the difference between anything you visualize and a real experience, so when you envision something you want, your subconscious mind starts working to make it a reality.

Moxie boards are a great tool to help you visualize where you're headed and keep the goals in your conscious and subconscious each day. We do so much firefighting every day that it's easy to lose sight of what we are actually working on. Gather a stack of old magazines, a pair of scissors, a glue stick, and a large sheet of cardboard. Flip through the magazines and cut out any pictures that represent to you your beat-the-alarm goals for a particular year or moment in your life. Paste the pictures on the cardboard in any order you'd like. Be sure to share your moxie board with a few Yaysayers and hang it somewhere so that you can see it every day. Schedule a sacred time each year to create a new moxie board, perhaps in January to start the New Year or on your birthday to start *your* new year. As part of her own LifeMoxie! 30-day Challenge, April spent time making moxie boards with her children one weekend. They each created their own moxie board, and the family ceremoniously hung each of them on the respective child's bedroom wall. They then sat down with their family calendar and began scheduling some of those dreams into reality.

When Jack Canfield and Mark Victor Hanson created the *Chicken Soup for the Soul* series in 1990, they too launched their dream by first visualizing their wild success. They were committed to reaching the New York Times bestseller list, so they printed the name of their book, cut it out, and pasted it over the number one best-selling book on the newspaper list. They posted their revised bestseller list where they could see it every day; with this vision they drove to success. By September 1994, *Chicken Soup for the Soul* hit number one on the bestseller list of the *New York Times*, the *Washington Post*, and *USA Today*. They have since sold over 100 million copies, created over 105 titles in the book series, and published the books in over 54 languages.

EAT THE ELEPHANT SLOWLY.

Start somewhere, just start taking actions. Imagine trying to boil the ocean or eat an entire elephant in one sitting. It's impossible. That's how we sometimes approach our beat-the-alarm goals and our missions. We wonder how we could possibly accomplish something that large, and it becomes so overwhelming that we give up before we even begin. Instead, break down your beat-the-alarm goals into many smaller beat-the-alarm goals like we practiced in LifeMoxie! Strategy #1, and then start taking some action on one of them.

Behind every success is an initial action in spite of fear. Every famous actress had a first day on stage unsure of her abilities; every famous rock band had a first day of practice together; every politician had a first day of campaigning; and every successful company experienced a first day of business unsure of its feasibility. There was a day when even Paul McCartney from the Beatles did not know how to play the guitar. What we don't often recognize when we see wildly successful people is that each of them started out in life without that wild success. They each had to learn their skill, create their fame, and build their fortune; and they did it by taking action.

Rock band U2 did not start out as the Grammy-award winning, Rock-n-Roll-Hall-of-Fame inductees that they are today. The band was formed in Dublin, Ireland in 1976 as a result of a notice the drummer posted on a high school community board seeking other musicians to form a new band. Two years later, four of the seven teenaged boys that answered the ad were still with the band. To get noticed, this fledgling band played cover songs in church halls throughout Dublin and introduced their original work to audiences in small doses. It was March 1978 when they won a talent show awarding them $500 and the requisite funding to record a demo of an original song. As a result of the award, they met their manager. Struggling for attention from audiences and critics in England and the United States, they played in local bars throughout these countries. Over time they created the following fan base necessary to make their album *The Joshua Tree* a smashing success.

While some stars are born into the spotlight of Hollywood, most celebrities start with merely a big dream and a lot of hard work, determination, and initial actions. A good-looking, charismatic but unknown entity, Brad Pitt left his journalism major at the University of Missouri and headed to Hollywood to follow his career ambition to become an actor. In between auditions, he wore a chicken suit for a fast-food joint, drove a limo, and modeled. Seven months after hitting the scene, Brad picked up roles on *Dallas* and *21 Jump Street,* and his career took off. Similarly Tom Cruise was a typical kid from Syracuse, New York. Plagued by dyslexia and bullied throughout high school, he found refuge on the stage and fell in love with acting. Skipping his high school graduation, he headed to New York City where he sat in on drama classes between auditions. Tom worked as a building superintendent to pay the rent before landing a small role in *Endless Love* and *Taps*, two roles that significantly launched his career.

Madonna Louise Veronica Ciccone, one of six children from a strict Catholic household in a Detroit suburb, similarly catapulted herself to stardom from nothing as a result of her determination, hard work, and moxie. After her mom died when she was 5 and her dad married their housekeeper, Madonna spent her teenage years in rebellion. As a harbinger to her success, she reinvented herself from a Catholic schoolgirl to a punk ballerina and landed a dance scholarship to the University of Michigan. In spite of straight As, she dropped out and headed for a work-study position at a dance company in New York City. After struggling for years as a dancer, working at Dunkin' Donuts, moving from one dive to the next, and living on popcorn, Madonna turned to music. Two years later she released her single *Holiday* followed by *Like a Virgin*, each a smash hit. Twenty years later, Madonna is still on the top of the power lists because she is constantly taking actions that keep moving her forward.

Former President Jimmy Carter also was not born into success or even into the political arena but worked his way to the Oval Office one position at a time. He began his political career by serving on various local boards that governed local hospitals, schools, and libraries. As his interest in making an impact through the government increased, he went on to serve two terms in the Georgia State Senate. He thought about running for the United States House of Representatives, but when a Republican entered the race for Governor, Carter, a Democrat, abandoned his congressional ambition in order to run for Governor of Georgia. While he lost the primary, he successfully prevented the Republican from winning. Carter spent the next four years planning for his next campaign for Governor, including making over 1,800 speeches throughout the state. He won the election and served as Governor for six years at the end of which he announced his plans to run for President. In the short span of nine months, Carter rose from an obscure public figure to President-elect.

MOUNTAINS OR MOLEHILLS.

We make mountains out of molehills when we build up some feat in our head to be so big that we are paralyzed from moving forward. To shrink a mountain down to a molehill, we just need to take one tiny step. Look at your beat-the-alarm goal and pick one of the smaller bite-sized-chunk goals you identified under that bigger beat-the-alarm goal. Just start there. What's one tiny move you can make that would get you closer to one of those goals? What if that tiny move became your goal for the day or the week?

Exercising is one of those molehills that we make into mountains that could easily become a molehill again. We tell ourselves that we need to go to the gym, we need to lose weight, and we need to become healthier. So we commit to exercising daily, drinking ten glasses of water, taking vitamins, eating salads, and cutting out sweets altogether. The molehill called "getting healthy" suddenly becomes a mountain called "change your entire lifestyle dramatically." We set ourselves up to fail before we even begin. Inevitably, we don't go to the gym every day or we enjoy dessert or we forget the water. The downward spiral begins. We tell ourselves that we'll make it up tomorrow by eating less, drinking more, and going to the gym for two hours. Let's face it, promising yourself that you'll go to the gym for two hours straight when you haven't gone once for the past six months has failure written all over it. When we don't go to the gym the next day because we don't have the two hours, the mental punishment begins. We decide not to go altogether because if we can't go for two hours then it wouldn't be worth it to go at all. Suddenly we have given up, and the journey hasn't even begun.

Arguably if we were 100 percent committed to changing our lives, we would not allow for any excuses; however, sometimes we need to set ourselves up for success first with small steps in order to create that 100 percent commitment. Little successes are like mini-wins that help us fortify our commitment. For example, committing to walk for 20 minutes around the neighborhood or the parking lot at work is a great way to start. Schedule your walk at a time when you know you can make it happen; for instance at the beginning of the day before everyone wakes up, during your lunch hour, or at the end of the day after work. Then eliminate other obstacles that could possibly get in your way. Lay out your clothes for the morning or pack a gym bag with your workout clothes to take to the office. If you are still feeling strapped for time, learn to multi-task. Read a book and bike; walk and listen in on a conference call; watch the news from the treadmill; plan out your day from the weight room. Literally take a step and discover how easy it is to fit 20 minutes into your day. Soon with a bunch of mini-wins, you will be ready to increase the 20 minutes to 30 and then to 45 or an hour. Suddenly, working out will become a part of your day's schedule like brushing your teeth, and you will begin scheduling other activities around your commitment to exercise.

The reality show *Amazing Race* pits 11 teams against each other in a 4,500-mile race around the world. During each show, the teams are presented with various challenges, and they race each other to be the first to complete that day's challenges. The participants scale mountains, swim seas, and engage in many other treacherous feats. They amaze themselves with their endurance, stamina, and prolific strength. These people are ordinary, untrained, un-athletic, everyday human beings who accomplish this race around the world by completing the daily challenges one at a time, each finish line driving them closer to the final finish line.

Your own beat-the-alarm goal, regardless of magnitude, can be broken down into manageable steps from which time frames can be established. Like the participants in the *Amazing Race*, identify the finish line for your race, bring along a teammate (or at least have a few Yaysayers), stay motivated and committed by sharing your beat-the-alarm goals and your missions, review your beat-the-alarm goals and manageable steps daily, and track your progress. What may at first seem like scaling a mountain will soon become a one-step-in-front-of-the-other journey.

Meghan, a LifeMoxie! client, wanted to revamp her business model to generate more revenue, but the thought of it became an insurmountable mountain in her head. As a result she didn't know what to do first, and so she didn't do anything week after week.

We sat down and looked at the mini steps that were required to get her from here to there. The most important change she wanted to make was to convert all of her clients from hourly billing to retainer billing. At first she saw this as one big project. As soon as we broke it down to converting one client a week, the weight was lifted from her shoulders. Meghan's eyes lit up when she realized that she could do this. We then made a list of every little step she needed to take to convert that first client—from writing a retainer contract, to creating a one-pager explaining the retainer model, to gathering that first client's phone number. Once the big project became a lot of little ones, she started making actual movement, which created the momentum she needed. Meghan confidently set a goal to have all of her clients converted by the end of the month at the rate of one client at a time. The mountain was shrunk to a molehill once again.

Another LifeMoxie! client, Virginia, wanted to run a marathon, but the thought of running a block exhausted her, and so her beat-the-alarm goal remained an untouchable mountain. In order to make the mountain into a molehill, we started with a few tiny steps. I met her outside her house one afternoon, and together we ran for one minute and then walked for five minutes, ran one minute and walked for five minutes, ran one minute and walked for five minutes. We continued this pattern for 30 minutes. Two days later we did the same thing. The following week she began running for two minutes and walking for five minutes. As the weeks went by she increased the running and decreased the walking. Each week that she continued to add minutes and mileage boosted her confidence. Within one month she signed up for the New York City marathon and the time frame around her beat-the-alarm goal drove her commitment forward. With cell phone in hand she called me from the finish line crying with pride at her own accomplishment.

You can use this same mountain-to-molehill approach to start moving on any commitment. Want to give up smoking? Commit to stopping for one day and then recommit the next day for one more day. Want to eat healthy? Try it for one day. Want to save money? Try an automatic deposit from your paycheck to a savings account for one month and notice how easy it is to live without the money. Want to learn to play an instrument? Practice for one day first and then make a new commitment. Want to change your job? Start by updating your resume. Whatever the mountain, make it a molehill.

Mix the Strategies.

It's a recipe. All strategies work together and if you want to know how to take a step, do it with all of the other strategies in tow. While asking is an important skill to have, it is but one ingredient in the moxie formula. The power comes from asking for what we need to achieve our beat-the-alarm goals while we act as if we have the right to ask, and we feel uncomfortable about asking all at the same time. You don't need to act as if you know everything. You need to act as if you have the right to ask, ask for what you need, stretch yourself enough that you are in uncomfortable territory, and keep moving forward.

John sacrificed his goals for his ego. He was so consumed with acting as if he knew everything and concerned that the other team members would find out that he didn't have all the answers that he ended up delaying the entire project because he didn't ask for help. John thought he needed to prove his place on the team. What he really needed to do was act as if he had what it took to be successful on the team and then ask for the support he needed to move it forward. Once he realized that "acting as if" and "asking" go hand in hand, John was able to jumpstart the team and his project to instant success.

Similarly, saying *Yes!* doesn't mean saying yes to everything. It means saying *Yes!* to those activities that pass the beat-the-alarm litmus test. Each time an opportunity is presented, ask yourself, "Does this further one of my beat-the goals or my missions?" We run around acting like being busy equates to being productive when in actuality it just means we're busy. To Shelly, for instance, being busy gives her purpose so she has become a "yes" person. She is unclear on the mission for her business, and to avoid doing the work that would transform her company from hobby to business, she keeps busy by saying "yes" to everyone and everything. As a result, she is scattered, chaotic, and frenetic. Shelly does great in the say-yes-now-figure-out-the-how-later department; she needs to do more work back in the beat-the-alarm department.

ACCOUNTABILITY.

Accountability is the mute button when excuses start flying. It's so easy to cheat when we are only answering to ourselves. "I'll floss tomorrow. I don't need it tonight." "I'll clean up the house tomorrow. I'm too tired today." "I'll practice tomorrow. My kids need me tonight." "I'll stop smoking tomorrow. I'm just too stressed out today." If taxes didn't come with a penalty, most of us wouldn't file them, or at least wouldn't do them on time even though the money contributes to social necessities we use each day, like roads and police protection. If grades didn't matter, the majority of us wouldn't study even though we need to learn skills to survive in the workplace. Penalties are merely instant consequences that hold us accountable, without which we are more likely to choose the immediate gratification of not flossing, not cleaning, not practicing, smoking, eating, drinking, not filing taxes, and not studying. In a world of instantaneous, it's hard to keep the long-term consequences on the radar screen.

When that first step (or even the second or third steps) is suddenly the hardest, it's time to call in the accountability troops. Whether it's one-on-one with another individual, or with a group of people, for instance, on a team led by a coach, it's important to find a structure to hold you accountable for taking the first step and keeping in motion. When you hire a coach for example, they will ask you to make commitments based on your goals. You can count on them to ask you each week about your commitments and whether you kept them. There are usually no immediate consequences or penalties for breaking your commitments; however, these structures remind you of the long-term beat-the-alarm goals you are jeopardizing by not fulfilling on your commitments.

A mastermind group is one form of accountability structure. Based on best-selling author Napoleon Hill's *Think and Grow Rich*, a mastermind group is a group of people who come together and meld their ideas and their thoughts for the greater good of the individuals. If you join a mastermind group, you are agreeing to allow the other members to hold you accountable, and in turn, you are making a commitment to the group to do what you say you're going to do, not cut corners or be run by excuses. These groups require that you create a relationship to your commitments that doesn't allow for your excuses. Without excuses, you become a powerful, driving, accomplishing force based on the commitments you make.

Book clubs, Toastmaster groups, and training partners are each based on commitments and accountability and will help you keep moving on some beat-the-alarm goal you have. In a typical book club, each month the members agree – commit – to reading a specific book and returning the next month to discuss it together. If you show up with excuses instead of your book read, there are no penalties; however, you will likely bring a bunch of excuses as to how busy you are. You may even be slightly embarrassed because you are left out of the conversation. The group may also feel disappointed because they were counting on your contributions to the conversation.

Employing a similar structure of meeting regularly and making commitments, Toastmasters groups focus on preparing and presenting speeches to work on speaking-in-public skills. Again there are no penalties for not doing the work, only the embarrassment of not following through when everyone else did. The group is counting on each of its members to be prepared to participate in some fashion, and when your only preparation is your excuse, it causes everyone else to shift and take on some of the responsibility that you failed to handle.

Finally, a training partner is another ideal accountability structure. A training partner is someone who is counting on you to show up, for instance, at 6:00 am to run, bike, walk, or work out at the gym. Often knowing someone is waiting for you is the driving force that has you get out of bed and take that step towards your beat-the-alarm goal of accomplishing the race. If we don't show up, we will have disappointed and inconvenienced another person. Because we are more apt to disappoint and inconvenience ourselves before another person, the mere fact you have a training partner may be enough to have you move forward in spite of your excuses.

I became an indoor cycling instructor because I needed an accountability structure to jumpstart my own workouts. I was struggling to wake up early enough to get to the gym before going to the office. I decided to become the instructor for the class that I was trying to wake up early to attend. Within a month I had obtained my cycling instructor certification, as well as the 6:30 am class at the YMCA three days a week. Knowing that a group of people were waiting for me compelled me out of bed extra early each morning. This structure forced me to listen to my commitment to my participants and ignore how I felt about getting out of bed.

Teachers are accountability partners. When you sign up to take a class, you are making a commitment to acquire new skills or learn about a new topic. The teacher creates a structure in which you will learn what you committed to learn. She then holds you accountable to learning by requiring that you turn in homework and take tests. The classes, the homework, and the tests are all structures of accountability. If learning something new is one of your beat-the-alarm goals, sign up for a class and be held accountable to learning it.

While an accountability partner needs to be a Yaysayer, a Yaysayer is not necessarily your accountability partner. When someone holds you accountable, you want them to approach the world from the glass is half-full perspective, but they do not need to be one of your own identified Yaysayers. On the other hand, just because someone is one of your Yaysayers does not mean that she will hold you accountable to doing what you say you want to do. For example, Debbie is Jill's friend and her Yaysayer. She is always encouraging Jill's ideas; however, while Jill wants to share her ideas with her friend, she does not want Debbie to hold her accountable. Jill is concerned with how that obligation may impact her friendship with Debbie. Instead, Jill hired a coach to play the role of accountability partner and Debbie continues to be a Yaysayer to Jill in their friendship.

Tap the Power of the People.

We have this notion that there is something wrong with us if we are unable to accomplish a task on our own. Men are often mocked for their quirky resistance to asking for directions. And women are so busy trying to prove they can do it all at the same time and all by themselves, that they forget to ask for any help. Why are we so afraid to tap the power of other people to help us get to where we are going? And why do we continue to keep doing tasks that we despise? If it's not fun, let's stop doing it and find someone else who wants to.

Tapping the power of the people in our lives enables us to generate the energy of a team and when we work with a team, standing still is not an option. First recognize that it is ineffective to do everything on our own. We don't always know how to complete every aspect of a beat-the-alarm goal, nor should we. For instance, if your goal is to write a book, don't spend time figuring out on your own the best way to get published. Someone else already has. Read their book or call them to help you.

Next comprehend the inefficiency of doing it all by yourself. We could accomplish more if we engaged others to assist us. For example, suppose that you are a consultant charging $50 an hour for your brilliant wisdom. Every month you spend four hours entering your income and expenses into QuickBooks to create your monthly financials, and you hate every minute of it. Now imagine you met a bookkeeper who could do the same work in two hours and charge you only $20 an hour. Hire this person immediately and stop wasting your life doing your own books.

Finally, you will discover that it is a lot more fun to accomplish a goal when you've enrolled others in the process. There is excitement and energy that gets generated among people as they work towards a goal together. Whether you are at work or at home, teams are powerful, especially when everyone on the team feels they're contributing to the overall goal.

David's goal was to throw a surprise party for his parents' anniversary. Overwhelmed with trying to do it on his own, he became resentful that his four siblings were not helping. Realizing that he never asked them to help, he scheduled a family conference call to share the idea with them. They loved it, and over the next three months, they created the party together over weekly conference calls, each contributing something to its overall success. Together they gifted their parents with a memory, and David's beat-the-alarm goal was accomplished.

Deciding who should be on your team is as important as recognizing the importance of having one. The first rule of thumb is to only allow Yaysayers on the team. They might not be from your identified list of Yaysayers, but they are Yaysayers in life. You don't have time to waste with naysaying on your team.

Secondly, think about what skills you currently lack that are needed to accomplish a particular beat-the-alarm goal. For example, when you start a new business you usually need a new web site, but that doesn't mean you need to become a web site programmer. There are experts out there who know how to do this very well already – find one and hire them.

Next, find others that share your passion. How can they contribute to your beat-the-alarm goal? Your own power increases exponentially when you start working with someone whose beat-the-alarm goal is furthered by contributing to your beat-the-alarm goal. For example, Jeremiah believes passionately in reducing our impact on the planet, and his beat-the-alarm goal is to start a local recycling drive in his neighborhood. To help him accomplish this goal, he recruited Bob, a neighbor who has been working to eliminate the use of plastic bags at grocery stores. Together they accomplished in a few short weeks what would have taken Jeremiah three months to complete on his own.

Finally, replicate yourself and double your productivity. What pieces of your beat-the-alarm goal can easily be handled by someone else? This will free up your time to be working on other aspects of your goal. You will get closer to your goal in half the time it would take for you to do it by yourself. For example, suppose you are a contractor and your beat-the-alarm goal is to renovate an old home to resell it. With your skills you could do this all by yourself, from the electricity, to the dry walling, to the painting. But if you hired a team of people to work with you, you could get the refurbished house on the market in a fraction of the time it would take to do it all by yourself.

One of the most important people to have on your team is a mentor. Whether it is your lifetime mentor, like Obi-Wan was to Luke Skywalker in *Star Wars,* or merely a mentor for a single project, engage mentors early and often. They are your role models. Identify people who have accomplished what you want to accomplish and have gone where you want to go, and then learn from them. Be a sponge; listen to their ideas; learn from their mistakes.

Never wait for a mentor to tap you on the shoulder and offer you guidance; instead, seek out people to be your mentors. Approach them with a proposal to create a mentoring relationship that clearly states what you need from them and what they'll get from working with you. For example, they may want to hone their own leadership skills or they may want to contribute to someone else's experience. In some situations, you may need to pay the person to be your mentor. If their connections, resources, or information are so valuable that it will help you get where you need to go, it may be in your best interest to pay for their time. In your proposal, be sure to include the goals you are working on and how often you want to meet with the mentor and for how long. The clearer you are about your needs, the better chance you have of creating an effective working relationship with your potential mentor. And know that one person will never serve all of your needs. Be prepared to work with many mentors over your lifetime to help you in the various adventures you intend to take.

In order to create a team that works well as individual contributors to you or well together as a group, be sure to identify each team member's individual beat-the-alarm goals. Understand what they need in order to show them how helping you will ultimately help them reach their goals. For example, if one member's goal is to make enough money to send his son to college and you are going to pay him for his time and expertise, you are contributing to his beat-the-alarm goals. If another member's goal is to learn event-planning skills, you are offering her an opportunity to do just that when you ask her to plan your event.

If the members on your team are working together as a team, be sure to engage them in collaborating on a team mission and a list of short-and long-term beat-the-alarm goals to further that mission. Make sure that they see how their individual missions, and beat-the-alarm goals are furthered by playing on your team. Only then will creating a team mission and team goals solidify the individuals into an effective team.

ELIMINATING TOXIC WASTE.

There is nothing worse than putting a team together with hope, expectations, and a vision, only to discover that one person on the team is toxic. Allowing this one person to contaminate the team hurts not only the momentum, but the team's excitement and energy. In order to keep moving, remove this person from your team immediately. It may be uncomfortable in the moment to do so, but as long as you stay focused on the team's current beat-the-alarm goal or their overall mission, being uncomfortable will pale in comparison to the damage this toxicity will cause.

LifeMoxie's teen leadership team should have removed one girl from the team who became extremely toxic to the team and its mission. She joined the team as a bright star who contributed her personality and excitement each week. But over time, her excitement turned to anger. Suddenly she began dumping negative comments into the conversation, snickering at other girls' contributions, and enrolling another team member to join her in the contamination. We discovered that her parents were going through a nasty divorce and that she had no apparent skills to deal with her emotions. Unfortunately, we allowed it to go on far too long and consequently, she impacted the energy and effectiveness of the team. We accomplished our goal but in the process we lost a lot of time, money, and excitement. We didn't have nearly as much fun as we had envisioned at the beginning of the journey. Had we been operating from a team mission we would not have tolerated her toxicity and we would have asked her to leave when the toxic waste became permanent and not just a temporary bad mood.

START FROM WHEREVER YOU ARE.

In spite of a powerful-beat-the-alarm goal, a Win file as thick as the dictionary, or a team of Yaysayers as big as a high school marching band, moxie requires movement, without which all other strategies will remain just good ideas. The other strategies are merely muscles, but it's movement that brings moxie to life. When we are stuck mentally and emotionally, we don't have the energy to move physically. In these situations, the best thing you can do is to stop listening to your feelings and start listening to your commitments. Allow your commitments to guide you; take some action, any action, regardless of how you feel. Start from wherever you are. It doesn't matter if you are starting new or if you are deep into the journey and suddenly find yourself stuck. Just create some forward motion, and the law of physics will take over. Maybe it's your first step in the direction of a goal; maybe it's your 47th step. Whatever it is, just start moving.

Tom Hanks' character in *Castaway* showed us the art of starting from wherever you are. As he boarded the plane late one night as a pilot for FedEx, he left behind a life rich with love, friendship, career, and a new fiancée. When the plane went down over the ocean, he was the only survivor. He stayed afloat until he found an island where he lived for four years until being rescued. Thinking he had died, the world he left behind went on without him. Upon his return he discovered that there was no longer room for him in that life he had. He was forced to start over from exactly where he was. He didn't know how he was going to survive on the island, and similarly he didn't know how he was going to survive back at home. In each instance, he had no other choice than to just move forward with action.

Talk is cheap except when we are talking about your life, then talk is expensive. When we talk about things we want to do in our lives but we don't take any actions that move us forward in that direction, we waste our time, energy, and emotions. We also waste other people's time, energy, and emotions when they are trying to support us. I talked about writing a book for five years and every year that I just talked and didn't move in the direction of my beat-the-alarm goal, I beat myself up for not accomplishing my goal. I even whispered the goal to a few Yaysayers who got excited and began supporting me long before I began to move. But I didn't do anything about it but waste all of our time and energy just talking about it. I learned quickly that talk may be cheap, but its impact on my life is always expensive.

How to Use This Strategy to Create Moxie.

Take your missions and your beat-the-alarm goals and craft a moxie board. Post your moxie board prominently at home or at work and continue to visualize your success. To make those beat-the-alarm goals a reality, start taking action – any action. One step at a time is all it takes to scale a mountain like a molehill. All the moxie strategies create moxie muscles but it takes action for your moxie to come alive. Find an accountability partner and create structures to support you in following through on your commitments. Tap the power of the people in your life to contribute to your beat-the-alarm goals and further your missions. Stop talking and start acting.

Exercises to Keep Moving

- Create a moxie board with pictures of your beat-the-alarm goals.

- What mountain are you standing at the bottom of wondering how to climb?

- What could you do to make it a molehill?

- Make a list of things that you talk about. What is one action you could take to put that talk into motion?

- What accountability structures can you put into place to support you?

- Who is on your team? Who needs to be on your team? Who needs to be off your team?

Life on Moxie

. . . .

MOXIE MOMENTS.

We've all experienced a moment when it felt like moxie just flashed across our life. We wonder how it happened, and we desperately hope that it will happen again. We got a taste of how moxie feels, and we want more – the burst of courage, the gumption, the near-bravado, the borderline brazenness. And it turned out so successfully. Bring that watch-out-world-here-I-come feeling back again! When we analyze the moment, we can see that we actually brought together all nine strategies in that one moment, often without intention. Maybe you were 5 years old; maybe it was last month. Regardless, we remember these moments, and we want more of them. We don't have to hope for them or cross our fingers and wish for them. Attracting them with our manifestations doesn't even create moxie. The power to create moxie is found only in our actions.

As you strive to create a life filled with moxie, start with a moxie moment. Work on creating that one moment using the nine strategies. Experiencing that one moment will give you the confidence you need to do it again. With the memory of that moment, the next one you create will come easier. After a while you will begin to create more and more moxie moments closer and closer together. Before long they will start to blend into each other until your life looks like one big moxie moment. Soon enough the moxie will be so ubiquitous in your life that you will not tolerate moments without moxie, and people will not recognize you without your moxie.

A top-notch scientist, Joey was terrified of speaking in public, but his mission for relieving pain had him creating one moxie moment and then another and another. He was offered the opportunity to present his research to a foundation to obtain additional funding and, never having done this, he hesitated out of fear. He eventually said *Yes!*, but panicked for weeks before the presentation. In spite of being uncomfortable, he kept the focus on his mission of relieving pain and his beat-the-alarm goal of funding the next phase of his research. Walking into the room with moxie, he asked for a million dollars. Joey was shaking inside but they couldn't tell. He asked powerfully and responded to their concerns, and the foundation awarded him with exactly what he asked for. One month later, he had another opportunity to present to a different foundation and this time he said *Yes!*, without hesitation. Soon Joey was creating opportunities to present his findings to anyone who could help him further his mission of relieving pain, while continuing to ask for money and support.

No Wishbone.

There are no wishbones in moxie, no lucky stars, no crossing your fingers, no lucky pennies, no secret. Moxie is created. Don't sit back and hope that a moxie moment hits you today. It won't. You have to create moxie. Moxie never comes accidentally, even if it seems like it did. Moxie is purely your creation. Victims hate this. They would rather count on luck or fate to define their lives. In fact, they create their lives around luck. They love to gamble, play the lottery, wish upon a star, pick up pennies, and count on many other superstitions to guide their lives. Victims spend more time wondering why nothing ever happens to them when their time would be better spent working to create moxie. With moxie on your side, you can make anything happen. Luck creates hope, but opportunity, possibility, options, and choices come only out of creating moxie.

One Size Does Not Fit All.

Moxie does not come in one size. Moxie for you will not be the same as moxie for someone else. The icons described in each of the nine strategies are offered as role models and inspirations, not as the standard by which you must create your own moxie. While a celebrity's moxie may ignite your own moxie, their moxie is not necessarily the benchmark for which to strive. Likewise, you cannot spend your time comparing your moxie moments with that celebrity's moments or even your friend's moments. The minute you think that your moxie moment pales in comparison, you lose the power that you generated with that moxie moment.

Your actions have to be bold, audacious, and brazen for you. That is, they might not be defined as bold and brazen for someone else, but moxie is defined in relevance to you and your experiences. A bold move for you may not be a bold move for someone else. What difference does it make? You are living your life, and they are living theirs. We each define our own moxie, and as such only you can define what is bold, audacious, and brazen. For example, if you are a recovering alcoholic, moxie for you may look like attending your first dinner party at which wine is served and declaring out loud for the first time "No, thank you. I'm an alcoholic." Or if you just completed your divorce, moxie to you may consist of asking your friends to set you up on your first post-divorce date. Or maybe you have been a nurse your whole career, and moxie to you may include signing up for classes to get a teaching certificate with the beat-the-alarm goal of becoming a high school English teacher. As you begin to experience wins, you will set goals that have you creating bigger moxie moments. For instance, if you are the nurse, you may create a moxie moment in which you walk into your boss' office to resign, and in the process ask for a letter of recommendation for your application to grad school or your application to teach at the local high school. Soon your moxie moments will inspire others who are just beginning to taste their own moxie.

In Between the Moments.

You've created a moxie moment. You're on fire. You are building up the confidence to do it again. But the space in between the moxie moments feels dark and lonely. What can you do in between the moxie moments? The simple answer is to start over. Whenever you are starting to feel sucked into the non-moxie abyss, go back to the beginning and spend time re-evaluating and articulating your missions. Tweak them or create new ones if your circumstances have changed. Recall that a mission is a purpose for an area of your life, usually an expression of your passions in that area. Then look at the beat-the-alarm goals you have defined around that mission. Choose one that you can drive towards immediately. Then apply the other eight moxie muscles to that mission and to achieving the beat-the-alarm goals that further that mission. In the chasm between the moxie moments, the best thing to do is to start working on the next one.

Feeling Stuck.

Feeling stuck is one of those states that we've all visited. Some people like to stay longer than others. Some send postcards. Some buy souvenirs. Others buy vacation homes. When you start creating more moxie in your life, you may find yourself driving through this state but you will no longer stay long enough to even buy gas. As soon as you recognize that you are feeling stuck, your moxie muscles will be so strong that you will do something immediately to propel yourself from this state.

Any reluctance you have for sharing with others about some part of your life is usually an indication that you are feeling stuck in that area. Perhaps you are not feeling confident about your choices; most likely you are not clear about your mission or you have not articulated any new beat-the-alarm goals. Think about a time when you were extremely clear about your mission and you were working on a goal that drove that mission. Remember how you wanted to sing about it from the mountaintops? For instance, suppose you are a senior in high school and you just got accepted to the college of your dreams. Your purpose for going to college is likely driven by some passion for the major you have chosen, a desire to earn a living, a longing to be independent, or perhaps a craving to change the world. Graduating from college with a degree is a goal that drives that mission. During your high school graduation party, everyone asks you what your plans are now that you have graduated. Proudly you tell them about college and your career aspirations. Now suppose a few years have passed since you graduated from college and you find yourself wandering from job to job, year after year. You clearly feel stuck, and when the 10-year high school reunion rolls around, you are conveniently unavailable. You have no idea what your purpose is anymore, and you don't know where you are headed. The last thing you want to do is talk to people about your life. The sad truth is that you have lost sight of your missions and the passions underlying them. As a result you are not pursuing any beat-the-alarm goals, and you certainly have no desire to share about any of this with others. You are clearly stuck.

Kelly experienced this hesitation to share when she was asked to raise funds for a charity race. She had signed up for a triathlon in Hawaii to raise money for leukemia. Although her heart does go out to those who suffer, Kelly's missions do not include finding a cure for the horrific and debilitating disease. Having no experience with the disease and no driving passion for finding its cure, she was having a difficult time asking people for money for the charity race. On the other hand, Kelly is extremely passionate about challenging adventures and staying healthy. The triathlon was a beat-the-alarm goal that furthered those personal missions, so she found it much easier to share with personal excitement about the race than to share about the fight against leukemia. Once Kelly shifted the focus to her own beat-the-alarm goal of completing the triathlon, she was easily able to share with others about the purpose of the race, and as a result, she raised over $5,000.

LIFEQUAKES.

Like earthquakes, lifequakes are those times when our life shakes us uncontrollably. My mom experienced a lifequake the year both of her parents and my dad passed away within eight months of each other, she turned 60, and my sister got married. Sometimes lifequakes happen to us, and sometimes they are a result of our poor choices. Many celebrities create their own lifequakes with their choices, which are then splashed on the cover of tabloids with details of their drinking and drug binges, cheating, and gambling. The true test of character for anyone in a lifequake is what they choose to do next. With moxie, they will repond; without it they will continue to flounder.

If you live in California, you're told to find a doorway under which to stand when an earthquake rumbles under your feet. The best thing you can do when a lifequake roars through your life is to build your moxie muscles and take actions – create those moxie moments. This is also the hardest time in which to create moxie because all we want to do is answer to our feelings and our circumstances, not create anything new. We wallow in self-pity and feel sorry for ourselves; we certainly don't want to think about what's next. When we feel stuck, moxie is a great remedy, but when we experience a lifequake, moxie is essential to getting us through it quickly. And while creating moxie may be challenging when we are feeling stuck, it absolutely tests us when we are in the midst of a lifequake. Regardless of how we feel, we need to start at the beginning and go through the nine moxie strategies.

USING ALL THE MUSCLES TO MOVE.

Just like your body needs all of its muscles to move, your life needs all of its moxie muscles to move forward. Whatever bold thing you want to do in your life, you will need moxie to do it. And in order to create moxie, you need to engage all nine strategies. Just celebrating your wins is not enough. Saying yes first without doing anything about it is not enough. Asking without doing something about the response is not enough. Acting *as if* in a vacuum is not enough. Even taking a few steps to move forward without the other muscles is not enough. To create moxie, you need to engage all the muscles. It's similar to baking bread. For the dough to rise and the bread to be edible, it takes all the ingredients working together. Without the yeast, it won't work. Without the salt, it tastes funny. Without the flour, it won't hold together. Moxie works the same way: all ingredients must be tossed in for the dough in your life to rise.

I have another goal just waiting in the wings, itching to be declared. I want to ride my bicycle across the country, from the Golden Gate Bridge to the Brooklyn Bridge. But to do this, I will need to create a little extra moxie. And to create the moxie to accomplish this goal, I need to engage all nine strategies.

Beat-the-Alarm Clock. First, while this is definitely a goal of mine, when it becomes a beat-the-alarm goal, I will know it. I will be getting up early not to write this book but to train on the bike. The goal of cycling across the country will drive me out of bed excited each day, ready to work on its accomplishment – it will literally become a beat-the-alarm goal.

Celebrate the Wins. It will be essential for me to celebrate all the successes I've had in my life, not only in cycling, but in physical adventures and personal challenges. I will need to constantly remind myself that I've done it before, so I can do it again.

Choose Your Channel. Surrounding myself with many Yaysayers will be crucial. I will identify my biggest Yaysayers and share my beat-the-alarm goal with them before anyone else. Then I will read books and magazines to learn from others who have done it before. I may even join a training club or find a training partner. I will also prepare for the naysaying – my own and others'. The naysaying is inevitable, but if I am not ready for it, the negativity may creep into my pores and impact my spirits.

Say Yes! First, Figure out the How Later. When this goal becomes a beat-the-alarm goal, I will say *Yes!* without waiting to figure out the how. I know I can figure out the *how* after I make the commitment, but until I make the commitment, I may hesitate.

Act As If. Act *as if* will definitely come into play to take this journey, especially when I meet Naysayers along the path who will question my decision. Acting *as if* will give me the confidence I need to declare the commitment and have conversations with people about the ride as if the journey is inevitable.

Respond, Don't Just React. I am cognizant that my journey will not go as I envision it and that along the way I will need to respond, not just react. Something might happen as I'm declaring this beat-the-alarm goal; something else may happen along the route. Instead of getting stopped by these literal and figurative potholes, I am going to keep responding with "What do I need to do next to get to the finish line?"

Ask. I will ask everyone for support, advice, guidance, resources, and cheerleading. I will ask powerfully and with conviction for my beat-the-alarm goal. The word *No* will surface somewhere, so I'll be prepared to ask, "What will it take?"

Be Uncomfortable. I'm not sure what is more uncomfortable – making a commitment to ride over 3,000 miles, or making adjustments in my life and business to accommodate my three-month trek. This adventure is laced with risk of failure and embarrassment, but when my goal becomes a beat-the-alarm goal, none of it will matter. Each time I feel uncomfortable, I will know that I have left the comfort zone in a quest for greatness.

Keep Moving. Without this, I have only a wish, a dream, a *someday.* The minute I start putting this into motion, with even the tiniest of actions, my beat-the-alarm goal will come alive! To keep moving will turn out to be the most important step in getting me off paper, out of my head, and across the country. If I look at this journey as 3,000 long treacherous miles, I may become overwhelmed by the daunting mountain at my feet, and I will likely miss the beauty and experience of the journey. Instead, I will take this on as one pedal, one mile, one town, one state at a time.

Your Turn. Are you ready to take a dream, a wish, a hope, a *someday* off the shelf, dust it off, and add a dose of moxie? Are you ready to feel alive again? Are you completely satisfied with your work, your business, your relationships, and your self? Or are you interested in creating a life that inspires and ignites you? The good news is that you always have a choice. The great news is that now you have the tools to help you when you do choose.

Oprah Winfrey, Lance Armstrong, Maya Angelou, Jim Carrey, Madonna, Jack Welch, Bill Gates. All of these amazing individuals have mastered the art of living. They were not born with success, fame, and fortune. But they are constantly working on it – one moment at a time, one choice after another. They have each experienced their share of failures, disappointments, lifequakes, and hardship. And in spite of these road bumps they continue to bounce back stronger than before. They define moxie.

They approach life with confidence, courage, determination, and boldness. They create missions and operate from a strength of purpose. They follow their heart and soul, not their circumstances. With spirit, courage, and grit, they move forward in the face of all that life throws their way. They have their share of Naysayers, but they are so focused on their missions and their beat-the-alarm goals that they choose to surround themselves with and listen to their Yaysayers. They recognize that the journey is never over — they are always working on their missions. As a result, they are rewarded with more fun, friends, freedom, money, opportunity, and adventure than people who do not choose moxie.

LIFE ON MOXIE.

We don't need to be rich and famous for our lives to be worth experiencing. We need to start taking actions and moving in the direction we want to go. Morpheus in the *Matrix* tells Keanu Reeves' character, "Stop trying to hit me and just hit me." Great advice! Let's stop wishing and start acting. Let's become bold, ballsy and bodacious — let's learn to create our own moxie.

We have a choice every day. We can *choose* the comfort zone. This is what other people do. They choose mediocrity. They answer to their feelings and their circumstances. They focus on their misfortunes. They carry their regrets, failures, and "somedays" with them like oversized baggage at the airport. Not people with moxie. We choose excellence. We slap wheels on our baggage. We create missions from our passions and stretchable beat-the-alarm goals that have us bounding out of bed most mornings. We celebrate our successes. We surround ourselves by Yaysayers, and we listen to them while muting the Naysayers. We shout "Yes!" to opportunities that move us forward in our missions and beat-the-alarm goals. We ask for what we need and want. We respond to objections. We bounce back quickly from disappointments, frustrations, and failures. We welcome the moments that make us uncomfortable because we know we are reaching for greatness. We approach our beat-the-alarm goals in bite-sized chunks, and as a result, we take leaps in our life. We are constantly moving forward. We embrace a challenge. We look for adventure. We know the choice is always ours, and at every turn we are choosing greatness.

LifeMoxie! Mantra

· · · · · · · · · · · · · · · · · · ·

Today, I am going to create Moxie.

I am going to be confident, courageous, determined, and bold.

I am going to feel adventurous, magnanimous, and unstoppable.

I am going to approach my life with tenacity and fearlessness.

I am going to operate from a strength of purpose all day.

I am going to follow my heart and soul, not my circumstances.

I am going to face any difficulty today with spirit, courage, and grit. I am going to move forward in the face of all that the day throws my way.

I am going to experience the day with vigor and possibility.

Opportunities for You to Jumpstart Your Own Moxie

- ## The LifeMoxie Challenge

  Work the LifeMoxie 9 Strategies Workbook and create your own LifeMoxie Challenge. Get ready to apply all that you've learned in this book with the workbook – a perfect way to get moving on your life. By working through each of the exercises outlined in the nine strategies, you can give yourself a kick in the pants and a kiss on the cheek!

- ## The LifeMoxie Book Challenge

  Jumpstart your dream of writing a book by putting your ambition on a mission! Infuse your dream with moxie and drive intentionally towards your beat-the-alarm goal of writing a book. We dare you!

- ## The LifeMoxie Keynote

  Want a dose of moxie in the morning? Just listen to Ann as she shares her favorite moxie stories with you in her LifeMoxie keynote.

- ## The LifeMoxie Mentoring Solutions

  Bring moxie to your company with the LifeMoxie Mentoring Program. Our unique approach to mentoring is peppered with moxie. Get ready to catapult your success at work through the only moxie approach to mentoring.

• THE LIFEMOXIE CONSULTING GROUP

We are people enthusiasts and behavioral specialists. By combining the art of management with the science of behavioral economics, we provide the emotional context required to create behavioral change. We develop real-world solutions that prepare middle leaders to implement high-stakes initiatives in complex, bureaucratic environments. We do this by intersecting people's commitment to serve with their commitment to success with their organization's battle cry. In the end we are committed to business-as-Unusual for life-as-extraordinary.

About the Author

From Silicon Valley corporate attorney to mentoring expert and advocate for business as unusual, Ann Tardy has never met a dull moment. Sally Jesse Raphael calls her "energetic!"

As the Founder and Chief Catalyst of The LifeMoxie Consulting Group, Ann combines the art of management with the science of behavioral economics to influence change and unleash moxie in people everywhere.

Ann first experienced the power of moxie while closing over $2 billion of venture-backed financings at two of Silicon Valley's largest law firms. Ann went on to lead the legal departments of two high-tech start-ups, taking one company public and the other to acquisition. Following her in-house tenure, Ann launched her own law firm, growing it to 75 loyal clients before merging it with a larger firm. While leading her entrepreneurial clients to success, Ann discovered that it's not willpower that separates the magnificently successful from the mediocre, but moxie.

In addition to dancing with entrepreneurs, Ann earned her moxie stripes as the volunteer Director of the Entrepreneurial Education program at a middle school, training 12-year-olds how to start and run businesses. And if that wasn't enough, she taught indoor cycling at the YWCA for seven years at 6:00 AM.

Ann passed the CPA exam while graduating with an accounting degree from the University of Illinois, Champaign-Urbana. She then graduated with honors from Chicago-Kent College of Law and passed the Bar exams in Illinois and California.

Ann was honored as an Outstanding Business Woman of the Year by the American Business Women's Association and honored with the Vanguard Award from The McGraw-Hill Companies for her contributions to their employees.

Ann is the author of:

LifeMoxie - Ambition on a Mission! 9 Strategies for Taking Life by the Horns

Moxie for Managers - The Secret to Evolving from Manager to Leader

Moxie for Mentoring - The Secret to Make Mentoring Matter

The LifeMoxie Consulting Group
www.lifemoxie.com
1.888.Ms.Moxie (1.888.676.6943)
27 Madison Ave. • Red Bank, NJ 07701

CPSIA information can be obtained
at www.ICGtesting.com
Printed in the USA
FSOW03n1209150217
30696FS